David Battie's

Guide to Understanding
19th & 20th Century British

PORCELAIN

David Battie's
Guide to Understanding
19th & 20th Century British
PORCELAIN

Including Fakes, Techniques and Prices

Antique Collectors' Club

British Library Cataloguing-in-Publication Data
A catalogue record for this book is
available from the British Library

ISBN 1 85149 123 6

Printed in England on Consort Royal Era Satin paper
from Donside Paper Company, Aberdeen, Scotland
by the Antique Collectors' Club Ltd., Woodbridge, Suffolk IP12 1DS

To Sarah, again

Probably CHAMBERLAIN'S WORCESTER c.1800
5ins: 12.8cm Red 'B' mark.
A pair of flower tubs and stands attractively painted with rabbits (a good subject) within gilt scrolls on a lemon yellow (a good colour) ground. The form is listed in the Chamberlain records as a 'Root Pot' and they were clearly intended to be planted up and not used as cache-pots. £3500–£4500

CONTENTS

ACKNOWLEDGEMENTS

My first thanks are due to Michael Turner with whom I co-wrote the first edition of this book. His death a decade ago profoundly affected all of us who knew him and he is sadly missed.

Thanks are due to all the staff at Sotheby's who have borne stoically my constant badgering for information or photographs, particularly Christina Donaldson for reading the captions and pricing. Thanks also to the photographers who took the photographs.

INTRODUCTION

The first edition of this book was published in 1975 and since then the market for 19th century porcelain has changed dramatically. Sotheby's Belgravia, the saleroom set up in 1971 specially to promote the then neglected Victorian works of art, had only scratched the surface of the market and a few freak sales gave an unbalanced picture of what was available to the collector. The first edition was a snapshot of its time, interesting, but much in need of refocusing. The most obvious difference, then and now, is the prices; many pieces have altered upwards tenfold, others are worth less than they were nearly twenty years ago. The greatest change has been a far wider base of collectors. *The Antiques Roadshow* has shown that it is quite possible for an unsuspecting owner to have in his possession a work of art he never considered was of any interest and which turned out to have significant value. The programme has prevented the whole-sale dumping of a house contents when an elderly relation has died and made the life of the 'knocker' much less easy. It has also suggested that a great deal of enjoyment could be had from forming a collection oneself. The huge rise in the numbers of car boot sales (now the most popular family activity on a Sunday), 'antiques' markets, fairs and shops bears witness to this. This large band of collectors is constantly seeking new fields of affordable collecting. As the field becomes established, new reference books are published to satisfy demand. Small factories such as Samuel Alcock, Charles Bourne and Machin now have devotees, whereas their products were rarely identifiable twenty years ago. Additionally, early books are superseded as research moves on. The first edition of this book listed nineteen titles in the Bibiliography; this edition has thirty-eight. In the light of new research, most of the captions have been re-written, some illustrations have been scrapped and new ones substituted.

EXPLANATORY NOTES

This book has been arranged according to the class of objects, rather than dealing with the pieces factory by factory. This should make identification easier if the factory is not known and the groupings make the factors which govern prices clearer. Within any group, the factories are arranged alphabetically, with the exception of some of the colour plates, and within that group are listed in chronological order.

BACKGROUND

This book starts with its roots firmly in the 18th century with wares from Derby, New Hall and Minton continuing the late 18th century Neo-classical style, or harking back to the mid-18th century Rococo. The Gothic revival, Empire, Renaissance, Japonism and others, all have their turn. The Victorians were wealthy, powerful and knowledgeable about earlier periods of design. They had the rare combination of technical proficiency, cheap and skilled labour and a rich consumer class prepared to buy modern decorative works of art of all kinds. Mass production meant that the lower classes could afford well designed and well-made objects for the first time. Unfortunately (and this is particularly true of the ceramics field) vast quantities of appallingly bad utilitarian ceramics were made to fulfil demand. These, made in large numbers, have survived in large numbers and have given Victorian works of art a bad name. Interestingly, since the early 1970s, these not-very-good objects have begun to fetch serious amounts of money and, because of this, a less jaundiced eye is being cast upon them. In 1975 Regency porcelain was acceptable, just; Victorian was still, to many, beyond the pale. It is hoped that this book will help to dispel any remaining doubts about the quality and interest of much 19th century British porcelain

BUYERS

It is possible to divide purchasers into five categories, although there may be a degree of overlapping. These are: the Collector, the Dealer, the Decorator, the Investor and the Joker.

The Collector usually specialises in one factory, style or period which he or others like him may have been collecting for years. He is probably obsessive, seeking to complete, as far as is possible, what he sees as a set or representative collection. This is in all probability a self-imposed limitation which may not be recognised by other collectors. On the other hand he may set off on a new track as one of the first of his kind. Sometimes a television programme, an exhibition or an article or book sparks off his interest in a subject. When enough new buyers appear, prices increase rapidly. The influx of new Collectors may upset the established Collector, who resents the newcomers muscling in on 'his' territory. His conversation or letters to magazines are peppered with phrases such as 'I remember when...' and 'Twenty years ago...'. Many of the old school will sell up, the prices having risen to a point where they are no longer prepared to buy. Their consolation is the tenfold increase in the value of their collection. The obsessive Collector, flush with funds, will then start again on another tack, lower down the price scale. Other Collectors will smile quietly to themselves, thinking how smart they were to have beaten the market. The Collector inhabits shops, from the meanest junk market to the Bond Street Gallery, usually sticking to a standard of venue in which he feels happy. In recent years the Collector has made his presence felt at auctions, either bidding himself, through an auctioneer or through a dealer.

The Dealer will be buying privately, from other dealers and at auction, and may well specialise in one type of object on which he may be the most knowledgeable in the country. Others are general dealers who may not know what it is that they are selling, but know what they can sell it for. At one time these general dealers provided a good source where the Collector or specialist Dealer could pounce on a missed 'goodie'. These lucky finds are now few and far between, as knowledge has disseminated through the market.

A strong player in the market, who was formerly only a minor factor, is the Decorator. He is not necessarily a professional, but the Decorator also includes the buyer who adds objects to his house (actually it is invariably a she) solely because it will 'look good' in the drawing room or wherever. The coffee can phenomenon is an example of this, see **Tea and Coffee Services**, page 204. For him, the factory, date and material are of far less interest than the impact the piece makes.

In this flurry of activity it is likely that several Collectors, the Dealer and the Decorator will at some point, perhaps a country auction, all be after the same piece. For example, collectors of hybrid hard pastes can cut across collectors of New Hall, and both may cross with the collector of teapots. The Decorator and the Dealer may also have turned up and all will be in the bidding, none wanting to leave without some token for their effort. It is this factor which can so distort country auction prices.

In the London auctions the Joker may appear. Completely unpredictable, his one contribution is almost unlimited money. He may be a passer-by who takes a liking to a vase or a particular period object and – on the spur of the moment – cannot live without his new-found love. Flamboyant bidding at the auction, to the annoyance of the Dealers, will ensure exceptional prices. Often the Joker's adoration fades in a matter of months and the market will return to normal – but not the prices. These may fall, but will still be higher than when the Joker appeared, as everyone has become acclimatised to the new level of prices.

Akin to the Joker is the Investor. Works of art, over a period of time, usually at least ten years, do make a good if not outstanding investment. This is public knowledge and the facts unarguable. Unfortunately, the antiques market is even more volatile than the stock market. When the money markets are humming, the money-man has spare cash over and above his house(s), car(s), yacht, stocks and shares and he will want to invest in works of art to go with his inflated lifestyle and to put away surplus funds. With all the skill of sticking a pin into the Shares Listing, he starts buying. He has little time and no taste and the galleries will unload on to him all the dogs which have been lurking in the basement for the right sucker to appear. He will also haunt the major auctions, sticking his hand up without really knowing why he is buying. His determination never to be beaten, which has made him such a success in business, is here his undoing. Two Investors bidding against one another will bring just the hint of smile to the most self-controlled of auctioneers. Unfortunately, as happened in 1991, the booming market will eventually collapse as the Investors decide to cash in their pictures, imagining that works of art can be sold like stocks and shares. Major works of art need to disappear for up to ten years for the market to forget them; in 1991 they were coming back in a matter of months and the market crashed. Money invested in works of art is bad money and in all likelihood a bad investment. The Collector who invests that most precious of commodities – time – is the one who makes a killing after a lifetime's collecting.

MARKS

The erratic factory marking, common in the 18th century, continued into the 19th, progressively diminishing. The reason for not marking is that ceramics were sold from retailers who wanted to repeat orders. If the manufacturer put his name to the piece, the retailer could be bypassed and a saving made. The exceptions were the factories with London or regional shops such as Barr, Flight and Barr's outlet in Coventry Street, London. A shop would have a stock pattern book and possibly some samples and the purchaser would make a choice from these. The order would be relayed to the factory and some time later the set would appear. To facilitate ordering, the pattern book was duplicated in the factory and each design was given a number. Once a book was full, a second was started and the usual format was to make the first designs therein 2/1; 2/2; 2/3 etc., and so on until, say, 2/999 when the next book was started at 3/1; 3/2; 3/3 etc. The numbers were painted on to the bottom of some, if not all, of the pieces in a set. Obviously a number of manufacturers were using the same system so that it would appear that pattern numbers are of no guide to a particular factory. Research is now beginning to unravel the numbers and possible attributions made. Godden's *Staffordshire Porcelain* (see **Bibliography**) has the best published list.

From 1797 a Copyright Act was introduced making it possible for a sculptor to protect his work. In 1815 the Act was changed so that any sculpture marked 'Published by...' followed by the details, could not be copied. The system included ceramic figures and jugs.

In 1842 the Design Copyright Act was introduced for two-dimensional work as well as shapes. This system did not supplant the Copyright Act and the two ran in tandem. An applicant (not always, but usually, a manufacturer) was given a lozenge mark with numbers which dated the application and gave protection for three years. It could be renewed. In this book, PODR stands for Patent Office Design Registration and the date given is the date of registration. The object should have been made within three years of that date. One suspects that some manufacturers were somewhat lax when it came to erasing the mark from a mould. The mark also enables the manfucturers to be identified. This can be done using J. and M. Cushion's *A Collector's History of British Porcelain* (see **Bibliography**).

In the 19th century many manufacturers, particularly in the second half of the century, took to date coding their pieces. These might be impressed or painted and were often fractional – $\frac{2}{78}$ meant February 1878; linear, 3:96 meant March 1896 – or in the form of a code or symbol. These are resolvable using Godden's *Encyclopedia* or factory monographs. It hardly needs saying but 'dates' on the bottom of pots are often not what they appear. Some are pattern numbers and some are the date that the factory claimed it was established (often years earlier than was the case). In 1891 the American McKinley Tariff Act brought the country of origin on to most ceramics, be it England, France or Germany. In 1902 the style changed to 'Made in England', etc. In the text, paintings which are signed are recorded thus: A(ntonin). Boullemier. This means that the actual signature on the piece reads: A. Boullemier.

BOWLS

Bowls were used far more commonly in the 18th century and earlier than they were in the 19th century or today. They were imported in large quantities from China and, to a lesser extent, Japan. What use they were put to can only be speculated, but probably soups, stews and gruel eaten with a spoon from bowls were more common than food on a plate. When tea arrived in the mid-17th century, it was drunk from handleless cups or tea bowls following the Chinese pattern. These are dealt with more fully in the section on tea wares, as are slop bowls and sugar containers. Large bowls were used in the 18th century for punch, but this had almost disappeared by the early 19th century. In the 19th century, bowls became works of art in their own right, copied from earlier examples such as Italian majolica. They were, however, usually in pottery, not porcelain. The same is true of the huge number of bowls surviving from bedroom washing sets, Exceptions were bowls meant for the display of flowers in the centre of a table, or for fruit.

It was only in the latter part of the 19th century that porcelain bowls appeared in quantity, particularly from Royal Worcester, followed in this century by Wedgwood's Fairyland lustre. The decoration of these, particularly Fairyland, suggests that they were never meant to be containers, but were solely decoration. Worcester examples which were plain on the interior were probably intended for fruit, others have matching salad servers. Bowls are amongst the most difficult objects to display and are generally cheaper than comparable vases, the exception being Fairyland.

'Pinging' a bowl with the knuckle to see whether it is cracked is not a reliable test. A jarring note will probably mean that the piece is damaged although some softer bone china bowls may only give a dull thud even if perfect. Conversely, a well repaired bowl may ring true. A very thorough examination is the only sure guide.

BELLEEK after 1869
Diameter 10ins: 25.6cm Impressed name, moulded PODR.
A rare and early Belleek table centrepiece, the lily buds and leaves tinted in pale colours. Belleek is a strongly supported factory with most interest coming from Ireland or the U.S.A.
£600–£800

COPELAND c.1870
Diameter 17¾ ins: 45cm Printed name.
A well moulded and large centrepiece, the white relieved by turquoise and gilding and stylistically typical of the period. Copeland made high-quality decorative and useful wares, often in Parian which they introduced in about 1843 as Statuary Porcelain. The large size of this piece makes it difficult to house, affecting the price slightly. The form would lend itself equally well to majolica.
£1000–£1500

ROCKINGHAM 1830-1842
Width 9ins: 23cm Printed griffin in puce.
A basket with a meticulously painted scene of Wentworth House, seat of the Earl Fitzwilliam, patron of the factory, within a burnished gold band and floral encrustation. The association of the subject makes this a great deal more expensive than would be, say, an unidentified church. Baskets such as this were placed inside the hallway for the visiting cards of callers. Several sizes are known and, with less interesting floral painting, prices start at £800–£1200.

WEDGWOOD c.1925
Diameter 7¼ ins: 18.4cm Printed vase and name.
A small bowl transfer-printed in gilding over streaky reds on a mottled blue ground. While the watery look was intentional it appears messy and is not popular. Dragon and butterfly subjects are still erroneously referred to as 'Fairyland', which they are not.
£100–£150

WEDGWOOD 1920s
Diameter 11ins: 28cm Printed vase and name, pattern no. Z.5360.
A bone china fruit bowl with flared sides, decorated on the interior with the pattern 'Garden of Paradise' in bright colours and gilding. Daisy Makeig-Jones, who designed the Fairyland subjects, gave them all names and each bears on the base a 'Z' and pattern number. Wedgwood is the name to conjure with in America, whence comes most of the demand. £1500–£2000

WEDGWOOD 1920s
Diameter 3¾ ins: 9.5cm Printed vase and name, pattern no. Z.5360.
A rare small bowl and cover with the pattern 'Big Eyes'. The printing is not as sharp as it could be, but the rarity of the piece will outweigh any production faults.
£1000–£1500

WEDGWOOD 1920s
Diameter 10½ ins: 27cm Printed vase and name, pattern no. Z.4968.
One of the commoner bone china Fairyland bowls with panels of brightly-coloured and gilt scenes. Pattern: 'Woodland Elves VIII'. Cracks in Fairyland pieces can be very difficult to detect as they easily pass notice in the complexity of the decoration. This also makes it easy to disguise restoration. A bowl has been noticed that had a triangular piece about the size of a 50p piece missing from the rim which was restored but still rang true when struck.
£1200–£1800

WEDGWOOD 1920s
Diameter 6¼ ins: 15.9cm Printed vase and name.
Despite the lack of fairies, this is still a desirable bowl, as fish lustres are rare. The background is mottled
blue with the fish coloured and gilt.
£300–£500

WEDGWOOD 1920s
Diameter 6¾ ins: 16.5cm Printed vase and name.
An uncommon bowl with a red-gold exterior and fairies in yellow-gold and tangerine enamel. The
interior in blue on a pearl lustre ground. Although generally expensive, there is considerable fluctuation
in price of the uncommon Fairyland types which do not conform to the usual format.
£800–£1200

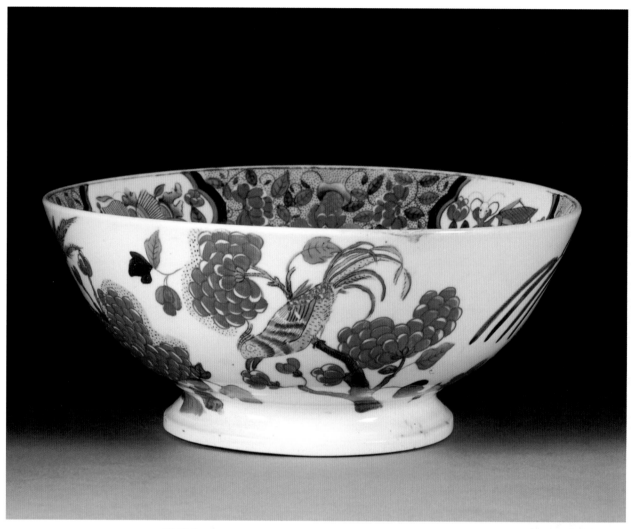

SPODE c.1810
Diameter 8½ins: 20.7cm No mark.
A rare bowl strongly influenced by Chinese *famille-verte* designs of the late 17th century. It fits perfectly into the Regency revival of chinoiserie which was as much Japanese influenced as Chinese. The pattern, a variation of 'Tumbledown Dick', was transfer-printed in black then hand-coloured in gilt.
£400–£600

JOHN ROSE, COALPORT c.1820-1825
Stand 10ins: 25.5cm Printed mark.
A 'Feltspar Porcelain' basket and stand well moulded and pierced with basketwork which reflect influences from Sèvres, Meissen and probably Swansea. The rose painting is of a high standard. Despite all this, the bowl is not a comfortable shape.
£600–£800

WEDGWOOD 1920s
Diameter 9¼ ins: 23.5cm Printed vase and name, pattern no. Z5447
A rare bone china bowl with the 'Hares, Dogs and Birds' pattern which was based on a Persian manuscript with the birds and animals in trees against a sea-green ground, the interior pearl.
£1000–£1500

ROYAL WORCESTER 1905
Diameter 9½ ins: 24.2cm Printed crowned circle mark and date code.
This salad bowl is typical of many reasonable quality but unexciting wares mass-produced around the end of the last century. It would originally have come with porcelain-handled, electro-plated servers. With them £300–£400. Similar pieces were made by a number of factories, including Moore Brothers in Stoke-on-Trent and by New York and Rudolstadt in Germany. However, in neither case would the quality or the price be as high (£150–£200). The New York and Rudolstadt mark is a crown above RW, possibly intended to mislead buyers into thinking they were buying Royal Worcester.
£200–£300

ROYAL WORCESTER 1905
Diameter 9ins: 22.8cm Printed crowned circle and date code.
A rather dreadful bowl with bad gilding and somewhat dirty-looking autumnal leaves and berries. The spider would put off purchase by arachnophobes. Produced by any other factory without the magic of the Worcester name it would fetch about half the price.
£350–£500

ROYAL WORCESTER 1882
6ins: 15.2cm Printed marks.
This teapot is inscribed on the base: 'The Fearful Consequences thro' the Laws of Natural Selection of Living up to One's Teapot.' It thus manages in one brilliant flash of humour to poke fun at the Aesthetes (the limp wrist and the bisexual lid); Oscar Wilde (the lily and the sunflower); the Grosvenor Gallery (which held an Exhibition of one blue and white Chinese teapot); Darwin (whose evolutionary theories were still under debate) and Gilbert and Sullivan (the greenery-yallery clothes). No other ceramic work of art of any period comes close to encapsulating the period in which it was made so effectively. There seems to be no record of why it was made and why it was made in porcelain of almost eggshell quality, making its survival in good state highly unlikely. Most have chips or restoration.
£1800–£2500

CABINET OBJECTS

This section includes all the small pieces, usually of exceptional quality, which were never intended for use. The Derby miniatures, page 28 are typical. Cups and saucers from services which have since been split up are included under services. There are devoted collectors of the small and fine who are prepared to pay over the odds for good examples and prices in this section may appear on the high side. It is arguable that many pieces illustrated in other categories should be discussed here as they were never intended for use.

Miniatures have been made by most civilisations, often as grave goods to provide the deceased with useful wares in the afterlife. In the 18th century, Chinese blue and white and coloured porcelain was imported in huge quantities and then copied by the English factories. Included were numbers of miniature vases known at the time as 'toys'. Whatever their pedigree, miniatures were neither apprentice pieces, nor samples; they were meant for the cabinet as a talking point or were made as playthings for children.

SPODE c.1820-1830
2⅜ins: 6cm high Painted red Spode and pattern number 4788.
An uncommon miniature teapot, well encrusted with flowers which have survived in fair condition. A desirable piece from the Spode collector's, miniature collector's and decorator's points of view.
£300–£500

BELLEEK c.1870
Length 13ins: 33cm Impressed name.
A masterpiece of clay latticework producing a basket and cover further encrusted with flowers and with crabstock handles, all under a shiny glaze. Very fragile and impractical, the handles are uncomfortably rough and the flowers sharp enough to lacerate oneself, but a decorative and much sought-after piece. Belleek is still making similar baskets by the same hand process, but the quality is less good. A modern example retails at several hundreds of pounds and a Second Period piece made after 1891 (when the word 'Ireland' was added to the mark) would fetch £1500–£2000.

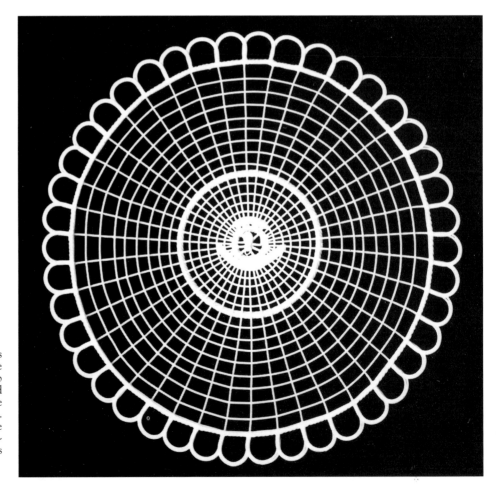

BELLEEK 1891-1926
10¼ins: 26cm
Applied impressed label mark.
The ultimate cleaning lady's nightmare. It appears in the pattern books as 'Spider Web Cake Plate', although it would seem unlikely that anyone would attempt to use it as such. Slightly disappointingly the design is arachnoidally inaccurate, the encircling strands are circles, not a spiral.
£1500–£2000

CHAMBERLAIN & Co. c.1815-1820
Painted name.
A good Empire-shaped cup and saucer with a gilt lattice on a salmon ground enclosing scenes of Ullswater Lake and Tonbridge Castle. At one time attributed to Thomas Baxter, such views could have been painted by a number of unidentified artists. Salmon-pink was one of *the* colours in the 1810-20 period. Chamberlain's started as a decorating studio, working on blanks supplied by Caughley. The quality is generally extremely high and prices are comparable with those of the main factory. Chamberlain & Co. became Kerr and Binns in 1852 and the foundation of the Royal Worcester factory. £700–£1000

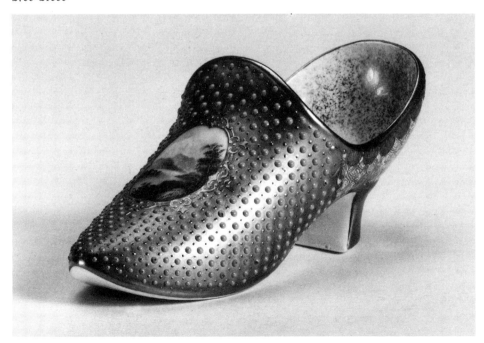

COALPORT c.1910
6ins: 15.2cm Printed crown mark and number V6353.
An uncommon 'jewelled' slipper, smothered with turquoise beads on a pink ground, the top with a landscape. £400–£600

25

WORCESTER, FLIGHT, BARR & BARR c.1825
5⅜ins by 4ins: 13.6cm by 10.2cm. Painted Flight Barr and Barr, Royal Porcelain Works Worcester, London House, 1 Coventry Street.
A fine pin tray very well painted with a Yellow Hammer and a Goldfinch reserved on a gilt seaweed ground. The form turns up with various decoration including views, feathers and flowers and there are also other forms of pin tray. Prices will vary according to type of decoration with shells, as always, the most expensive. £1200–£1500

ROYAL CROWN DERBY c.1900
11ins: 28cm Printed crowned initials mark, incised 448.
A fine cabinet ewer painted by D(isere). Leroy, signed. The best Derby pieces of this date rank amongst the most meticulous of the period, Leroy's always being extremely finely executed and rare. Not infrequently the craftsmanship is more apparent than artistic merit.
£2500–£3500

ROYAL CROWN DERBY c.1910-1920
Heights 1¼ ins to 3¾ ins: 3.2cm to 9.5cm Printed crowned monogram, pattern nos. 1128 and date codes.
The mass-production of miniatures by companies advertising them as 'Collectors' Editions' has swamped the market with thousands of meritless pieces. This has not dampened the enthusiasm for Derby examples. The fact that they are transfer-printed with one of the two Japan patterns makes for a coherent collection. There is a wide range of shapes, some of which are rarer than others. Additionally, every piece can be dated from the code on the base. Prices from £150–£700

ROYAL CROWN DERBY 1912
Height 6¼ins: 15.8cm Printed crowned monogram and date code, pattern no.1128.
This table bell is not common, nor is its miniature version, which would fetch about the same price. The flowers are in iron-red, blue, green and gilding. £200–£300

GEORGE GRAINGER & Co. c.1840
Height 9½ins: 24 cm Printed name.
An uncommon biscuit porcelain bower being bedecked with glazed and coloured flowers by cupids. Because of the delicate nature of the encrustation it would be difficult to find in good state. With a few leaves damaged £500–£700

ROCKINGHAM 1831-1842
Width 3⅜ins: 8.5cm Griffin in puce and C1 2.
A rare dressing-table box, the lid moulded in the shape of a butterfly and in natural colours, the base in azure blue edged in gilt.
£800–£1200

ROCKINGHAM 1831-1842
Height 3¾ins: 9.5cm Printed griffin in puce.
A miniature teapot with a rustic green handle and applied coloured sprays of flowers. An uncommon object which, with the magic of the Rockingham name and mark, results in a high price, despite the almost inevitable nibbling of the flowers. A pristine example would make £400–£600

ROYAL WORCESTER possibly 1876
Height 9½ins: 24cm Printed mark and blurred date code.
A well made and decorated 'Japonaise' tea kettle with good quality decoration in bright enamels and gilding. It could have stood on a tray such as that on page 108. Japanese taste was better understood at Worcester than at any other English factory including Minton. This despite the influence at Minton of Dr. Christopher Dresser, whose designs were more abstract and more influenced by China than Japan. In the first edition of this Price Guide, the comment was 'typically underpriced' – still true. £250–£300

ROYAL WORCESTER 1878
Diameter of saucer 3¾ :ins: 9.5cm Printed crowned circle and date code.
A Japanese taste cup and saucer probably not made as a cabinet item but making its way there rapidly as the difficulty of drinking from an angular cup with too small a handle became apparent. The handle is formed of a chocolate and gilt dragon.
£80–£120

ROYAL WORCESTER c.1880
Impressed crowned circle.
A double-walled cup and saucer, honeycomb pierced, enamelled and gilt and applied with turquoise beads. Introduced in the 1840s, it was copied from Sèvres which was in turn inspired by Chinese *linglung* or Devil's work. A service was exhibited at the Great Exhibition of 1851 by Chamberlain and another set given to Jenny Lind after her concert for the benefit of the Worcester workers. She refused it on the grounds that she could receive no payment for a charity performance. Such pieces were probably the inspiration for George Owen's work, see page 31. A jug of the same type would make £300–£500.

ROYAL WORCESTER late 19th century.
Height 5ins: 12.7cm Impressed crowned circle.
A double-walled teapot by George Owen, but not signed, with turquoise and white beading on coloured grounds and gilt details. Although of good quality, the lack of Owen's signature makes all the difference to the price. With signature £2500–£3000.
£1500–£2000

ROYAL WORCESTER 1890.
Height 6⅜ins: 16.2cm Printed crowned circle.
A well pierced vase by George Owen but, like the last, lacking his signature. A printed gilt facsimile of Owen's signature has been noted applied to an unmarked piece. With genuine signature £2500–£3500.

ROYAL WORCESTER 1907
Length 6½ins: 16.5cm Printed crowned circle, date code and incised signature.
A rare slipper by George Owen, with exceptionally sharp cutting and good gilding. An ideal cabinet object. Shoes may seem a curious object to be petrified in ceramic, but they come from a long tradition. The Dutch and English both made them in the 17th century in Delftware. They were given to newly-weds to bring fertility and were made in their thousands in the Victorian era, particularly in Germany. Few are more than £20 or so. £3000–£4000

ROYAL WORCESTER 1919
Height 6½ ins: 16cm Printed gilt mark, date code and incised signature.
A very elaborate box and cover by George Owen. Despite the fact that the knop has been broken off and stuck back, it would still be very saleable.
£3000–£4000

ROYAL WORCESTER 1970s and 1939
Jug 1½ins: 3.8cm Printed crowned circles and date codes.
Royal Worcester miniatures are popular and less common than Royal Crown Derby, although, generally, of a lower standard of production. The jug is by William Powell. Thimbles issued in sets in the 1980s and 1990s by lesser factories and sold by mail order are only a few pounds a time and are unlikely to see any return on the investment for a century or so. Thimble £100–£200. Jug £200–£300.

CACHE-POTS & JARDINIERES

The terms cache-pot and jardinière are often treated as synonymous, whereas they each have a distinct function. The cache-pot hides the terracotta pot of a growing plant, whereas a jardinière is a decorative container in which to grow plants. The latter has a hole in the base for drainage and usually comes with matching stand, the former has no hole. The American term for both is planter.

In the 18th century oval bowls with wavy rims, known as Monteiths, were made to suspend wine glasses in to cool them. Although the practice had died out by the 19th century, some were still made in the same form for flowers.

Surprisingly perhaps, ice cream and iced desserts were great favourites long before the introduction of the refrigerator. Ice was cut in winter and stored underground in ice houses in which it would last the year round. After making the dessert it was brought to table in an ice pail. This was a cylindrical vessel which held crushed ice and salt surrounding a separate container in which the dessert was held. The deep cover also held ice. The dessert and 'pud' course warranted the richest service and most ice pails were made to match. They are now very saleable in pairs as decoration for the sideboard.

BELLEEK 1870-1880
Diameter 10ins: 25.5cm Printed symbol and name.
A good cache-pot with crisply modelled flowers at the mouth, the sides with moulded prunus blossom. Several petals are missing, as is almost inevitable, but a perfect piece £800–£1200.

PROBABLY COALPORT mid-19th century
Diameter 4ins: 10cm Simulated Sèvres mark.
The form was originally made at Vincennes in 1753 as a *seau à bouteille* or wine bottle cooler but these were more likely to have been sold as cache-pots by Coalport. The painting is heavily influenced by Sèvres, both in painting and gilding. Furthermore, Coalport paste at this date is very similar to Sèvres' and there is every reason to believe that they were made to deceive. At this date, many English factories, including Coalport and Minton, were working on undecorated Sèvres blanks which had been sold by the factory at the beginning of the century. The quality is extremely high and such pieces, which are not uncommon, are expensive, £1000–£1500. However, a comparable pair of originals would be in the region of £8000–£12,000.

COALPORT mid-19th century
Diameter 9ins: 22.8cm No mark.
This jardinière is based on a Sèvres original and has been quite well painted with rather angular exotic birds, possibly by John Randall who worked at the factory from 1835-81. The *bleu-de-roi* ground has unusually good gilt borders. Randall was famed at the time for his Sèvres-style birds, which are actually easily distinguished from the originals by their thin, spiky quality and thin, watery enamels. This gives the birds a translucent quality, unlike the solidity of the originals. He worked both on blanks from English factories and on Sèvres originals. A feature of Victorian reproductions of Sèvres bird painting is the tendency to include three or more birds rather than one or two. £800–£1200

MOORE 1868-1875
Diameter 10ins: 25.4cm Impressed name and retailer's mark.
 A well cast jardinière with waterlilies against a turquoise ground, the neck with black and gilt key-fret. This is better quality than most of Moore's production, much of which is in the white, exposing a finely-crackled glaze over the creamy body. Moore's had trouble with their bone china body and many pieces are stained brown. The retailer's mark of Thomas Goode's may account for the high standard. £500–£700

ROCKINGHAM c.1830-1842
Height 6½ ins: 16.5cm Printed griffin in puce.
A very rare pair of cache-pots attractively and delicately painted with panels of flowers enclosed by gilding on a deep blue ground. Rockingham was one of the few factories at the beginning of the 19th century which satisfactorily combined the prevailing Empire style with the neo-Rococo. £2000–£3000

UNATTRIBUTED c.1820
Height 5ins: 12.7cm No mark.
This spill vase could have been made by one of several factories and the form, without the feet, is frequently seen. The additions are uncomfortable and make the piece resemble a miniature paraffin stove. The decoration is loosely based on a Chinese famille-rose original which has in places been misunderstood. Small spill vases such as this were always sold in pairs, if not a garniture of three, and they look very lonely on their own. Pair £500–£700.
£200–£250

ROYAL WORCESTER 1899
Diameter 13¾ins: 33.5 cm Printed crowned circle, PODR and date code.
A large cache-pot with well cast, high relief green and brown lion masks and scrolls against the usual yellow/apricot ground. Size is important in the price of jardinières, the larger the better. £500–£800

ROYAL WORCESTER 1901
Diameter 14ins: 35.5cm Printed crowned circle, date code.
Another large cache-pot, printed and coloured with flowers on a yellowish ground, the shoulders with shallowly-moulded panels of masks and scrolls lightly gilt. A similar example entirely hand-painted with flowers would fetch £1000–£1500 and with Highland cattle by J.Stinton £2500–£3000 .
£600–£800

for companion panel see below.

Mr Asher Wertheimer

Copy of Le Paul

MINTON early 20th century
This page from the extensive Minton archive shows just how good the painters of the time were at imitating Sèvres. The style of painting is slightly more 'overblown' than the original, but is very close. There is a possibility that the Minton artist used the work of the Sèvres artist Le Doux as an original. We no longer know why this bowl was copied; did Mr Wertheimer want a pair for himself, or was he intending to pass them off to someone else as genuine?

UNATTRIBUTED c.1850
Width 14½ins: 36cm Pseudo-Sèvres interlaced Ls.
One of a pair of good ormolu-mounted jardinières, the bowl, a Sèvres original, well-painted with flowers reserved on a gilt-pebbled (*caillouté*) *bleu céleste* ground. These Sèvres blanks, decorated in England, can still cause disagreements between experts. This one would not be open to question as the ground does not exist at Sèvres. There the pebbles are much smaller and were only used on a dark blue ground. Many of these fakes, for that is what they are, come complete with impossible painter's and date marks. Either the decoration was never undertaken by that particular painter or the date code corresponds to a time when the painter had not joined the factory or had left. Nevertheless, this is a splendidly decorative pair of jardinières.
£4000–£6000

FIGURES AND BUSTS

Figures were amongst the first objects produced in Europe after the discovery of true (hard paste) porcelain by Böttger at Meissen in 1708. They have remained popular ever since. Their appeal is obvious, which is the criticism levelled at them by the collector of wares. In the 19th century, figures ranged from the severely neo-Classical through the Rococo revival and on to the sentimental pieces of the late Victorian era.

At the beginning of the century, the shepherds and shepherdesses of the 18th century were still in favour, as were putti. Derby particularly hung on to the former style longer than most and there must have been a ready sale, as large numbers survive. Derby was also the factory that came closest to Sèvres in the production of biscuit porcelain, now out of favour. Oddities such as the Minton flatback figures were presumably not popular as few have survived, more of their figures 'in the round' are known. Both of these are of exceptionally fine quality with decoration second to none. It may be that they were simply too expensive to have a ready sale.

During the Regency, animals were popular, particularly dogs and deer, although a wide range is available. These have remained perennial favourites and are strongly collected today.

During the reign of the rarely mentioned William IV, Staffordshire factories began issuing portrait figures. Many of these were of bone china and therefore fall within the scope of this book, but the Staffordshire portrait figure collector makes no distinction between pottery and porcelain, and only a few have been included. P. D. Gordon-Pugh's book covers the subject fully (see **Bibliography**).

In the middle of the 19th century Copeland and Minton developed a new body. Statuary Porcelain (Copeland) or Parian (Minton); the latter name has stuck. Largely used for figures, there are also some exceptional wares produced in Parian. It was all the rage in the second half of the century, encouraged by the various Art Unions which offered Parian as prizes in their lotteries. While white porcelain is not usually a strong seller, Parian is an exception with, as always, nude figures being the most popular. Oddities are not uncommon. Raphael Monti's 'Veiled Bride' has risen from about £30 when the first edition of this book was published in 1975, to over £1000 today.

Doulton figures have been another success story, although these fall into this century, not the last. The numerous different models and the huge variety of colour variations ensure a collecting field that ranges from about £30 upwards to £1000+. As with stamp collecting, a comprehensive book is a vital tool in assessing any figure and this is provided by *Royal Doulton Figures* (see **Bibliography**).

The most dramatic change in figure collecting over the last twenty years has been the collapse of the Limited Edition market. To quote from the 1975 edition: 'It is now quite possible for an edition to be over subscribed, completed and for an example immediately offered for sale to rise in price from £1,500 to £11,700 – as in fact happened with the (Royal Worcester) Ronald Van Ruyckvelt doves.' The same doves, back on the market in 1993, would probably only fetch the original price, if that. It should be a warning to those seduced by Sunday colour supplement advertisements into buying 'Collector's Plates' (whatever that means). They will have no investment potential and are no more a work of art than the photographic reproduction of them in the magazine.

SAMUEL ALCOCK & Co. Possibly 1827
Height 8½ins: 21.4cm Printed beehive and name.
A fine and rare pair of busts of George IV and his brother Frederick Augustus, Duke of York. They may have been made to commemorate the latter's death in 1827. They are uncoloured and unglazed but the plinths are glazed and with gilt lines. Busts of this quality and of this date are uncommon and are mainly collected by devotees of portrait and commemorative wares. This pair would also appeal to those interested in ceramic history as they were withdrawn shortly after issue for 'the infringement of certain rights'. £1200–£1800 pair

SAMUEL ALCOCK & Co.
1840-1850
Height 7½ins: 19cm Printed and impressed name.

A small and attractive pair of Parian groups of fine quality, the complexity of the modelling indicating that a large number of moulds would have been employed. Uncommon anyway, perfect examples are very rare and few pieces of Parian appear with the Alcock name. Stylistically they are akin to 18th century Sèvres biscuit porcelain models. The subjects are appealing and there would be strong demand from both decorators and Parian collectors. £500–£700

BELLEEK c.1870
18¼ins: 46cm Printed mark
A large and rare Crouching Venus based on a 1st century Roman marble in the collection of Her Majesty the Queen, itself based on an original of c. 250 B.C., now on loan to the British Museum. This example was restored about the feet. Perfect £1200–£1800. £600–£900

JOHN BEVINGTON 1872-1892
Length 8¾ins: 22.2cm Painted JB in underglaze blue.
These fruit dishes are well modelled and coloured copies of Meissen. Bevington was one of the smaller Staffordshire factories and it specialised in good copies of other, earlier products, mostly after Meissen. They were also one of the few in the 19th century to copy loosely the Meissen crossed swords mark (another was Minton). Unmarked examples can be distinguished by the slightly creamy colour of the bone china which usually has a fine crackle to the glaze, quite unlike the Continental hard paste.
£600–£800

WILLIAM BROWNFIELD & SONS Last quarter of the 19th century
Height 9¾ins; 25cm. Impressed name.
One of a pair of figures entitled Mama and Papa depicting children dressing up in their parents' clothes, the boy in top hat, boots and with an umbrella. The Victorian attitude to children can, at times, be a mite sickening, but this pair has a certain charm. Contemporary Continental copies are known but they are much less well made, £40–£60.
£400–£600

CHAMBERLAIN c.1828
Height 5ins: 12.8cm Painted name.
A very rare set of the Tyrolese group of singers, the Rainers, who toured England in 1827 and 1828. Some sets were marked, others were not. Although, in most cases, unmarked porcelain is worth less than marked, here it would make no appreciable difference. The set originally sold for £2 10s. Single figures now £400–£600.
£2200–£3000

COPELAND post-1847
Height 12ins: 30.5cm Impressed name, printed title.
An early and uncommon Parian figure of Narcissus after John Gibson R.A. and so entitled. It was modelled by E. B. Stephens for the Art Union of London as Copeland & Garrett's first successful Parian figure. Fifty copies were produced, all to be given as prizes in their lottery. An example of this early edition £800–£1200.
£600–£800

COPELAND 1860s
Height 13ins: 33cm Impressed name.
A scarce group of Florence Nightingale tending a wounded soldier, a ribbon at her breast inscribed 'Scutari' and with the title impressed from type on the base. This example has a broken hand and stick, accounting for the low price. In good condition £700–£1000. It would appeal as much to commemorative as to Parian collectors. The original marble by T.Phyffers was exhibited at the Royal Academy in 1857.
£400–£600

COPELAND 1861 *14⅛ins: 36cm Impressed marks including factory, sculptor's name and date and Art Union.*
The original marble 'Veiled Bride' by Raphael Monti was one of the most popular Victorian sculptures, as was its Parian counterpart. It is so once again and prices have soared in recent years. £1000–£1500

COPELAND c.1865
Height 16¾ins: 42.5cm Impressed and printed names.
The famous 'Tinted Venus', after John Gibson R.A., holding her golden apple. The original marble aroused a storm of protest as the sculptor lightly coloured her for the 1862 London International Exhibition. This Parian reduction was issued by the Art Union of Great Britain, but it balked at ordering her tinted, adding only gilt details. £400–£600

COPELAND 1862
Height 17¼ins: 44cm Impressed name and date.
Victorian sculpture and Parian figures can be over-sentimental to our eyes or be quite charming, like this group which is entitled on the base 'Go to Sleep'. The original was by J(oseph) Durham for the Art Union of London, both pieces of information cast into the base. £300–£400

COPELAND & GARRETT 1833-1847
Height 7¾ins: 19.7cm Printed and impressed name.
An uncommon pair of 'Feldspar porcelain' busts of John Locke and Ben Johnson. Feldspar porcelain was one of the many new bodies introduced between the beginning and middle of the 19th century, in this case by Josiah Spode about 1820. These busts are no great advertisement for the material, since they both display an unfortunate blotchy discoloration. An unspotty pair £700–£900. £400–£600

DERBY early 19th century
9ins: 23cm.
A curiously muddled figure of a Pan-horned white child with a cornucopia of Spring but intended to illustrate Africa. The whole style is 18th century in concept and Derby lingered on with the Rococo long enough to meet it second time round in the early 19th century. Minor repairs and a firing crack have reduced the figure from £300–£400. £180–£250

BLOOR DERBY c.1830
Crown and D in red, the elephant with pattern no. 34. The pair of peacocks is richly gilt as is the saddle-cloth of the elephant, which has a grey-brown skin. Both are uncommon but these examples were damaged.
Elephant £600–£800 perfect
         £400–£600 damaged
Peacocks £800–£1200 perfect
         £400–£600 damaged

BLOOR DERBY c.1826
6¼ins: 16cm Printed red circle mark.
A rare figure of Madame Vestris as a Broom Girl. Madame Vestris was an actress who appeared at the Haymarket in 1926 to great acclaim. The piece is based on a lithographic music cover published in the same year.
£400–£600

ROYAL DOULTON 1924-1938
Height 7¾ins: 19.6cm Printed mark, HN 597 and painted title.
A typical Naughty Twenties figure entitled 'The Bather', removing her brilliant purple, blue-lined robe to reveal her tinted skin. This model went through several changes of coloration, eventually ending up with a black painted bathing costume.
£400–£600

ROYAL DOULTON c.1914-1938
Height 7ins: 17.7cm Printed mark in black, HN 35, script titles.
A portrait figure of the actor W.S. Penley taking the part of Charley's Aunt in the play by Brandon Thomas of the same name. It opened in 1892 and ran for 1,466 performances. The figure was designed by Albert Toft. The double interest from Doulton collectors and those interested in the theatre would ensure a high price.
£400–£600

ROYAL DOULTON 1929-1949
Height 8ins: 20.3cm Printed mark, HN 1341 and painted title.
An amusing figure evocative of the period entitled 'Marietta' and based either on the heroine in *Die Fledermaus* or on the 1910 musical *Naughty Marietta*. It was modelled by Leslie Harradine and in this version has a bright red collar and mottled red interior to her cloak. Doulton figure collecting is almost impossible without Eyles and Dennis' book *Royal Doulton Figures* to guide one. There were so many variations of colouring and so many different models, that making general statements is difficult. On the whole the more evocative of the period the piece is, the more likely it is to be sought after. Those that were issued for only a short period before being withdrawn are more likely to be rare than one that sold over a long period. As always, a pretty girl is more desirable than an ugly man (although the latter tends to be rarer).
£500–£600

GOSS & PEAKE 1867
Height 26ins: 66cm Incised names.
A rare and large Parian bust of Charles Dickens. Goss was only working for a short time with Peake, a roofing tile manufacturer. William Gallimore, who modelled the bust and whose name is also incised on the back, left Goss to work at Belleek in 1863 along with several other workers, but returned to continue with Goss. The demand for large, decorative pieces of sculpture together with a popular subject would ensure a high price.
£1000–£1500

W.H.GOSS c.1880
Heights 16½ ins and 17ins: 41.9cm and 43.2cm Printed name.
A well cast and rare pair of figures with refined coloration and gilding. Expensive, as they would be much sought after by both Goss and Parian collectors, as well as being suitable for the decorator's market. £1000–£1500

JAMES HADLEY & SONS 1903
Height 9ins: 23cm Printed crowned circle mark, date code.
A well modelled and coloured group in shot silk enamels and gold after James Hadley. The character on the left is Paulus Kruger, the Boer leader in the Transvaal and the other The Right Honorable Joseph Chamberlain. They were probably made to commemorate the defeat of the Boers in 1900. Similar groups include other contemporary politicians.
£500–£700

MINTON c.1826-1828
Heights 5½ins and 4¾ins: 14cm and 12cm No mark.
A very rare pair of figures which pre-dates the familiar Staffordshire 'flat-back' examples. The backs follow the contours of the front and are hollow at the rear. Don Quixote has a loop to accommodate a wooden or metal lance. The modelling and colouring are of a high standard like all Minton figures of this date. The spelling of the name varies. There are six others in the series and they represent the earliest known Minton figures.
£1500–£2000

MINTON c.1835
Height 7½ins: 19cm No mark.
A pair of well-coloured and gilt figures with a great deal of charm and based on Meissen originals. They are considerably rarer than are 18th century Chelsea gardeners, for example, but much less expensive. Watch for restoration to early Minton figures; they seem particularly vulnerable to damage.
£700–£900

MINTON c.1835
Height 9ins: 23cm No mark.
The same as the preceding figures but here forming candlesticks with encrusted flowers and elaborate
bases. The normal variations of casting, positioning and painting make little difference to the price, but
a major elaboration such as this will.
£2000–£3000

MINTON c.1830
Height 8¼ins: 21 cm No mark.
A well-decorated figure of a Spanish guitar player, model 94 in the pattern book, seated (rather oddly) on a Chinese garden seat. This, like the last, is illustrated in *Minton*, where the size is given as 7¼ins. The player should be accompanied by a dancer, £1000–£1500.
£500-£600

MINTON c.1840-1850
Height 6¾ins: 17cm No mark.
An early Parian figure following the tradition of biscuit porcelain. With the companion male figure, £500–£800.
£250–£300

MINTON c.1835-1840
Heights 3¾ins and 4ins: 9.6cm and 10.1cm
No mark.
A rare pair of candle-snuffer figures, their clothes brightly coloured and gilt. They were made to fit on the base of an elaborate bower candlestick and a pair complete would make £2000–£3000. They are illustrated in *Minton* along with the original drawing from the Minton pattern book – any such illustration will increase the value of a piece.
£1000–£1500

MINTON c. 1840
13¾ins: 35cm.
A naturalistically modelled greyhound on a claret and gilt cushion. Although dog models are generally very saleable and the quality of this piece is good, it has a couple of problems. One is that, at over a foot high, it has transcended the divide between 'dinky' (and attractive) to lifelike (and unappealing). Another is that bits of it are all-too-realistically modelled. Although unmarked, the model appears in the Minton pattern book as number 130: 'Large Greyhound'.
£700–£1000

MINTON c.1845-1850

Height 13¼ins: 33.6cm Incised ermine mark.

An early Parian group of Naomi and Her Daughters-in-Law, a copy of which was on view at the 1851 International Exhibition. Large models in good condition are very sought after but damage affects the price dramatically. Matt, chalky-white Parian, more akin to biscuit porcelain in appeerence, can be simulated by restoration quite successfully but that of a warmer tone with a smear of glaze is a great deal more difficult.

£700–£1000

MINTON 1858

Height 13¾ins: 35cm Impressed Minton and date cypher.

A Parian portrait figure of Sir Colin Campbell, Lord Clyde, by John Alexander Paterson McBride and dated 1858. Sir Colin served in China, India and the West Indies, commanded a division in the Crimea and suppressed the Indian Mutiny. He is shape 346 in the design book and is not to be confused with Colin Minton Campbell, shape 501.

£300–£500

MINTON 1955
Height 6ins: 15.3cm Printed crowned globe and titles.
Three from a set of ten of the Queen's Beasts after originals by James Woodford O.B.E., R.A., themselves based on stone orignals made for Henry VIII at Hampton Court. The figures are brightly enamelled and gilt and were issued in sets in an edition of 150 in 1955 at a cost of £175. They also formed part of the Coronation (1953) Vase made from contributions by all the major Staffordshire factories. The set appreciated considerably up until the 1980s. With the flood of so-called 'Limited Editions', the market has all but collapsed. In the first edition of this book they were priced at £650-£700.
£1500–£2000

ROCKINGHAM 1826-1842
Height 3⅞ins: 9.8cm Impressed Rockingham Works Brameld, Incised No 136 and C1 2 in red.
Many Rockingham and Derby animal figures are all but identical, probably because the Rockingham factory hired Derby modellers. The incised numbers vary, however, and, in the absence of any other mark, serve to differentiate the factories. Rockingham pugs and cats are the most frequently found, although not common, but peacocks are exceptionally rare. This model is uncoloured but for green patches on the base and gilt details. At one time almost any early 19th century porcelain animal was attributed to Rockingham, particularly if it had shredded clay 'fur'. It is now known that Rockingham never used this technique.
£500–£700

ROBINSON & LEADBEATER 1884
Height 17½ins: 44.5cm Moulded signature.
A rare, well cast and coloured tennis player with the moulded signature of R.J.Morris. Sporting figures are popular with collectors, who usually collect any material connected with the subject of their devotion. They are, in descending order of desirability: Golf, Tennis and Cricket. The others are of much less interest. If this were simply a figure of a man, without the racket it would be worth only £150–£250. With a lady partner without racket, £400–£600.
£400–£600.

ROBINSON & LEADBEATER c.1885
Heights 14ins and 14½ins: 37cm and 36.5cm Impressed initials.
A decorative pair of Parian figures of Italian children, well cast, coloured and gilt. Robinson &
Leadbeater was one of the few Staffordshire factories to colour its Parian, which is invariably of a high
standard. The results resemble coloured Continental biscuit porcelain, although the latter are more
brightly coloured. Robinson & Leadbeater's coloration usually has an autumnal feel to it. Most pieces
are marked at the rear, rather than on the base as is usual, but many are not marked at all.
£700–£900

ROCKINGHAM c.1831
Height 7⅞ins: 19.4cm Griffin in red and incised No. 42.
Rockingham figures were produced in both biscuit and coloured form. This figure of Napoleon in green coat with gilt braid epaulettes and medals and red cuffs and collar is very rare, as are most Rockingham figures. There would be multiple interest in the figure from Napoleon collectors (of which there are large numbers), commemorative, and Rockingham collectors. In all probability this is, in fact, a theatrical figure of John Warde taking the part of Napoleon Bonaparte in a play of the same name which opened in 1831. Yet another collecting category could, therefore, be added to those interested.
£600–£800

ROYAL WORCESTER probably c.1862
Height 12ins: 30.5cm Printed crowned circle.
These Parian busts were originally produced during the Kerr & Binns period, 1852-62, and may have been issued to commemorate Albert's death in 1861. The crown was not added to the Worcester circle mark until 1862. Along with other busts and figures of the period, they are generally of good quality. They are also known with turquoise beading and gilt details £800–£1200.
£700–£1000

ROYAL WORCESTER 1865,
Heights 7½ins and 7¾ins: 19cm and 19.8cm Printed crowned circle.
A pair of spill vase putti in the 'Ivory Porcelain' body, which was a glazed Parian. Pieces were coloured in soft enamels including a reddish-purple supposedly akin to Capodimonte, of which there is a vague hint in the technique. They are not popular as the faces are generally unattractive. This particular pair has the strong disadvantage of looking downwards, making them difficult to display – a further minus point.
£300–£500

ROYAL WORCESTER c.1870
Heights 10½ins and 11ins: 26.7cm and 27.9cm Impressed crowned circle.
This pair of girls wear powder-blue and gilt dresses clinging to their uncoloured bodies. The models were called 'Before the Wind' and 'Against the Wind' in the pattern books. Considering the extraordinarily strait-laced nature of Victorian society it is remarkable how many sculptures of the period are of naked or barely clothed figures. They can, like many figures of this date, be found coloured £1000–£1500, in Celadon £800–£1200 or white £500–£800.
£800–£1200

ROYAL WORCESTER 1886

Height 6½ins: 16.5cm Printed crowned circle, date code.

A figure of a Russian, one of a series symbolising ten countries of the world, modelled by James Hadley and first issued in 1881. This example is in tinted ivory, but they can also be found white or fully coloured. It is not uncommon to find date codes on sets of objects such as figures or services, with the codes differing by a year or two. As pieces came off the production line they were stored on shelves and orders were made up as and when required. It would be easy for some pieces to be pulled from the back of a shelf and married to more recent production. This *should* make no difference to the price, but collectors can be fickle.
£200–£300

ROYAL WORCESTER 1874

Height 6¾ins: 16cm Impressed crowned circle and PODR.

One of a set of six menu-holder figures of down-and-outs (shape 440) which, although not particularly rare, are very sought after. Although presumably only issued in sets, some seem rarer than others, the illustrated example being the commonest. The set was introduced in 1874 (the year of this example) and underwent variations of colour over the years. White £100–£150; reasonably coloured as this one £150–£200 and very good at £200–£300, for single ones.

ROYAL WORCESTER 1888
Height 8½ins: 21.6cm Printed crowned circle and date code.
One of a pair of so-called Kate Greenaway candlestick figures
modelled by James Hadley and named after the popular Victorian
book illustrator whose children were dressed in a vaguely Empire style.
There are probably about thirty different figures, several forming
candlesticks. They were a huge success at the time and are perennially
popular. Pair £800–£1200, uncoloured £500–£700.
£300–£500

ROYAL WORCESTER 1889
Height 6¾ins: 17.3cm Printed crowned circle, PODR, date code.
A sweetmeat basket figure, palely coloured. At first glance this figure
could equally be Minton, Brownfield or Moore, when it would be less
expensive. A pair £500–£800.
£250–£300

ROYAL WORCESTER 1891
Heights 11¼ins and 12½ins: 28.5cm and 31.8cm Printed crowned circle and impressed marks.
A good pair of Turkish water carriers decorated in 'Shot Silk' enamels and complete with bowls and the detachable liners which are usually missing. Modelled by James Hadley, they are amongst his most popular figures. Shot enamels are gold sprayed onto a coloured ground giving an iridescent effect. As with most Worcester figures, the quality can vary.
£800–£1200

ROYAL WORCESTER 1892
Height 8½ins: 21.5cm Printed crowned circle, date code and PODR.
Described in the factory shape book as 'Bringaree Indians', although they look more like Turks. A good
pair, in 'Shot Silk' enamels, but not uncommon. In white £400–£600. £600–£800

ROYAL WORCESTER 1898
Height 19½ins: 49.5cm Printed crowned circle and date code.
A rare figure of 'The Violinist', shape 1487, of large size,
coloured in 'Shot' enamels and gilding. Figures such as this
would appeal as much to the interior decorator as to the
Worcester collector. Damage to the violin, for example, or
a restored hand, would reduce the price by about 5-10%.
£1000–£1500

ROYAL WORCESTER 1898
*Height 21¾ins: 55.5cm Printed crowned circle, date code and
PODR.*
A large and well-decorated figure, her robe in gilt-sheened
green on a blue-tinged base. The large size and the fact
that she is supporting something on her head make her
ideally suited to conversion into a table lamp. There is,
however, no central hole for the flex and an example
drilled for electricity would reduce the value by about 10%.
Damage on a suitable case for conversion to another
purpose affects the value less than on a cabinet piece.
£1200–£1800

ROYAL WORCESTER 1899
Heights 12ins and 12¼ins: 30.5cm and 31.1cm. Printed crowned circle, date code and PODR.
These figures of musicians are palely enamelled and with gilt flower scrolls. Any figure with fine detail such as fingers free-standing, should be carefully checked for restoration as the soft tones of Worcester are far more easily simulated in restorer's paint, than glazed white.
£600–£800

ROYAL WORCESTER 1911
Height 25¼ins: 64.2cm Printed crowned circle, date code.
An exceptionally large figure of the 'Bather Surprised', shape 486, which was made in three sizes of which this is the largest. Another ideal interior decorator's piece, suitable for most rooms in the house or conservatory.
£1500–£2000

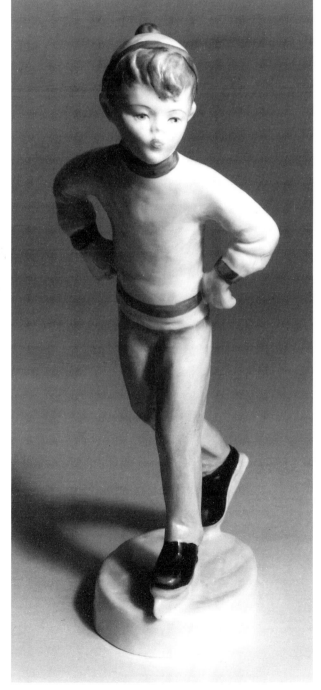

ROYAL WORCESTER 1919
Height 9¾ins: 24.8cm Printed crowned circle, date code.
An example of 'soft' moulding and uninteresting gilding, otherwise an attractive figure. A sharp, tinted example £300–£500. This is a late casting of a figure originally issued in the 1860s, one of a pair of 'Joy' and 'Sorrow', this being Joy. At the end of the Great War, the ceramics factories had lost most of their skilled workers and quality was poor until others could be trained. A good pair would be £600–£900.
£200–£300

ROYAL WORCESTER 1930s
Height 8½ins: 21.5cm Printed crowned circle.
One of a series modelled by Freda Doughty, Dorothy's sister, and representing the days of the week, a boy and girl of each, this is Tuesday's Boy. Others include the months of the year and nursery rhymes and some are still in production. In common with most post-war figures, rarer examples are shooting up in price.
£100–£150

ROYAL WORCESTER
1930s
Height 7ins: 17.8cm Printed crowned circle.
A rare pair of Art Deco figures of 'Victorian' musicians from a set of four, modelled by Ethelwyn Baker in 1931. Very much of their period, these '30s figures have recently become collectable. Generally the British factories were less influenced by the Art Deco movement than those on the Continent.
£800–£1200

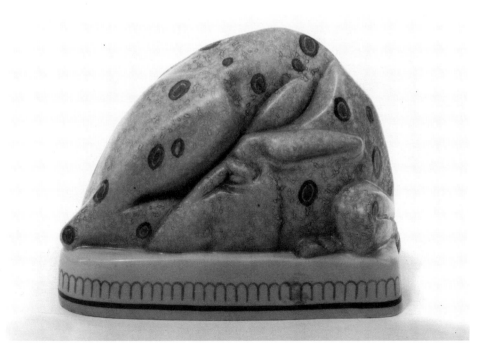

ROYAL WORCESTER
1931
Height 5¼ins: 13.3cm Printed crowned circle mark and date code.
An Art Deco model of a sleeping doe issued in 1931 and modelled by Eric Aumonier (shape 2874) a freelance artist working in the early 1930s. It is enamelled in grey-blue and emerald and, apart from being a rare figure, it is one of the most successful in the style. It bears some kinship with the Worcester reproductions of Japanese netsuke. These are also rare and fetch £150–£200.
£300–£500

ROYAL WORCESTER 1933
Height 5½ins: 14cm Printed crowned circle, date code, painted title.
'The Old Goat Woman', after a model by Phoebe Stabler, brightly coloured and uncommon. The pattern number on the base of this figure does not fit with the shape book, the correct number being 2886, not 2896, which was a calf by Stella Crofts. Such mistakes are not common but, unlike the stamp market, do not add to the value.
£500–£800

ROYAL WORCESTER 1935
Height 9ins: 22.8cm Printed crowned circle, title, date code.
A pair of figures of King George V and Queen Mary, modelled by Gwendolin Parnell and coloured by Daisy Rae, in an edition of about 72 to commemorate the Silver Jubilee. The edition was intended to be of 250 but the series foundered when the King died. They are, for Worcester, rather poorly executed, but for the collector are desirable for their rarity.
£1000–£1500

ROYAL WORCESTER post-1938
Height 3ins: 7.8cm Printed crowned circle.
This group of leopard cubs from a series of 'Zoo Babies' modelled by Doris Lindner was issued in 1938, but did not prove popular. Examples are rare.
£400–£600

ROYAL WORCESTER 1937
Height 9½ins: 24.5cm Printed crowned circle, date code.
An example of Dorothy Doughty's rarest bird models – the 'Indigo Bunting on a Plum Twig'. Made to be a cheap Christmas present, its lack of flowers and foliage resulted in a market failure with only six or seven being made. See following also.
£600–£800

ROYAL WORCESTER 1958
Height 10¼ins: 26cm Printed crowned circle, facsimile signature, date.
A fine pair of 'Canyon Wrens on Prickly Pears', attractively modelled and coloured and larger than most of the American series. These groups have considerable logic to their being in limited editions. Limitations were originally introduced by printers when hand printing, to ensure that copies of special books or prints were not marred by damaged or worn type or plates or by slackness by the press men. In the case of Dorothy Doughty birds and most pre-1980 models, the same logic applies: the standard of hand construction and painting could only be maintained through relatively short runs. The mass-produced 'Limited Editions' of today are without logic and they have destroyed the demand for the real thing. This pair were worth about £3000-£5000 in the 1970s. £700–£1000

ROCKINGHAM c.1826-1841
3⅛ins: 8cm red enamel C1.! incised No. 142 and 1 size.
An attractive and rare monkey eating a nut. The model number does not fit known examples or the recorded extent of Rockingham figures up to 120. Man's nearest cousins are perennially popular and this would appeal to a wide range of collectors.
£500–£800

ROYAL WORCESTER c.1880
10¼ins: 26cm high Printed marks.
A pair of so-called 'Kate Greenaway' figure candlesticks coloured in the usual peach tones and gilding. All Worcester figures of this kind are slip-cast quite thinly, but are nevertheless robust.
£600–£900

ROYAL WORCESTER 1967
Height 9½ins: 24cm. Full printed marks including title, facsimile signature and date.
A model of the famous racehorse Arkle, modelled by Doris Lindner and coloured chestnut and brown with silver shoes. It was one of an edition of 500. Before the edition was completed it was already selling at a premium at £2000. The fame of a racehorse is very ephemeral except with race-goers and stud owners. This, together with the collapse of the limited edition market, accounts for its dramatic fall in price. £300–£500

ROYAL WORCESTER 1968
Height 11½ins: 29.9cm Full printed mark, facsimile signature and date.
This model of Prince Philip on a Polo Pony was modelled by Doris Lindner and issued in an edition of 750. The reins of the horse are applied subsequent to firing with Araldite which is then hardened in a low temperature oven. They will, therefore, appear as restoration under an ultra-violet (black) light. This is true of many figures and a knowledge of how the factory constructed the piece is vital if they are not to be condemned unfairly as restored. £400–£600

UNATTRIBUTED mid-19th century
13½ins: 34.3cm Unmarked.
An anonymous but good quality Parian naked bather. This example displays its Sèvres biscuit porcelain origins and is akin to models by E-M. Falconet. A mark or attribution would help the price by about 20%. £300–£400

ROYAL WORCESTER 1881

6ins: 15.2cm approximately Printed and impressed marks including shape numbers, PODR for 1881 and date code S.
A part set of the popular Countries of the World modelled by James Hadley and from the first year of production. They were sold in white (unpopular today £400–£600); tinted, as here (the most satisfactory) and fully coloured (rarest, but perhaps less ceramically satisfying £1000–£1500). £800–£1200

UNATTRIBUTED second quarter 19th century

Poodles 3⅝ins: 9.2cm.
The red splodged dog at the rear has a lop-sided plaintive look which would appeal to a ceramic animal collector, as would the flanking poodles and their pups. These have a regal stillness and despite their poor modelling would be very saleable. Cats are far rarer than dogs and are equally popular. The example here may be Derby, although sorting out which factory made which model is complicated even with the aid of Rice's book (see Bibliography). Single dog £150–£200; pair poodles £300–£400; cat £250–£300.

ROYAL WORCESTER 1968

Height 6¼ins: 15.8cm Printed crowned circle, title and facsimile signature.

A group entitled 'Charlotte and Jane', after a model by Ruth van Ruyckevelt, one of a then popular series of Victorian figures issued in editions of 500. This cost £290. In their heyday in the 1970s, many editions were oversubscribed and were selling at a premium before delivery was taken. All Worcester limited editions came with a Certificate, often wood framed, and this must be present or the price will fall.

£400–£600

UNATTRIBUTED c.1850-1860

Height 10ins: 25.4cm No mark.

A typical Staffordshire portrait figure and, like many, in porcelain not, as many people assume, in pottery. Generally those made before the middle of the 19th century are better moulded, better painted and better titled. The very dark blue of the poetess's bodice is typical, as is the name impressed from type. Staffordshire figures are another whole subject (see Pugh, Bibliography) and Eliza Cook is only given here as an example.

£250–£300

JUGS, MUGS AND EWERS

Of all domestic crockery, the average 19th century household probably had more jugs than anything else. There were no milk bottles, cans of beer and often no tapwater. The latter was served at table in a jug, the milk and cream were measured into one's own jug from the milkman in the street and ale was fetched from the inn in one's own jug. Large numbers have survived, mostly in pottery and of little merit, but fine examples in porcelain were also made.

The jug (or more often mug) could serve as an appropriate vehicle for the retiring present of a worker or overseer of a factory, the name and date often being added in gilding. Both also commemorate weddings and christenings. The jugs and mugs are often well painted with flowers and are fashionably decorative. Later in the 19th century, and more commonly in this, the commemorative mug was issued for coronations, royal weddings, jubilees and so on.

In the first half of the 19th century, some fine moulded and coloured jugs were made by Spode, Ridgway, Coalport, Minton and almost all the major manufacturers of the period. They reflected all the current styles including Sèvres, Neo-Classical, Rococo, Empire, Gothic and, at times, amalgams of all these. Whether these hybrids 'work' or not is a matter for personal taste, certainly they can be quite amusing. The moulded jugs and mugs, more frequently made in stoneware, were occasionally issued in tinted Parian or bone china. They will make much the same price as the stoneware examples, despite being rarer. The ewers made for washing sets are very rarely in porcelain although Spode, for one, made some splendid flower-painted examples. They are now highly prized for their decorative qualities.

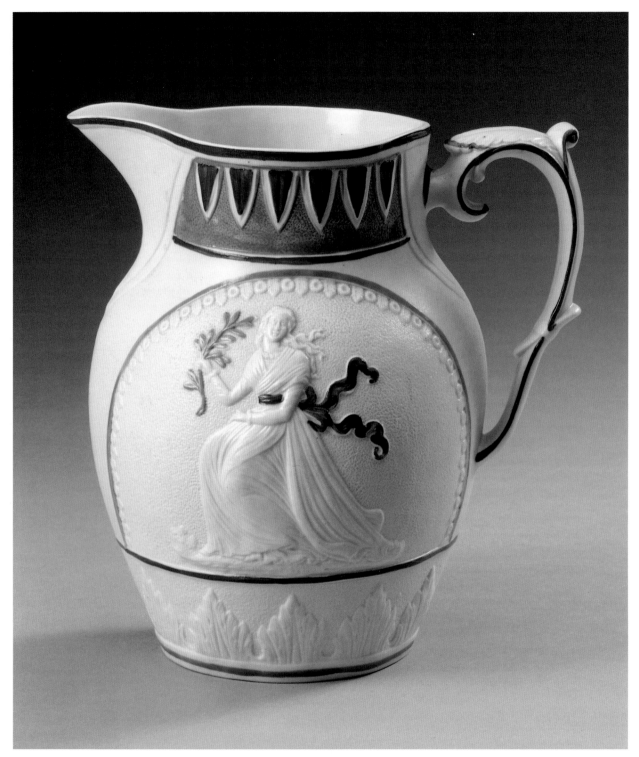

CASTLEFORD type c.1800
Height 7¼ins: 18.5cm No mark.
This jug is included largely to be provocative. In about 1790 a fine white stoneware was developed, possibly at the Castleford Pottery, south of Leeds. It was a feldspathic (or felspathic) stoneware with a smear glaze and was often more translucent than bone china. It would, therefore, seem to be more akin to feldspar porcelain than to stoneware. It is easily confused with Parian ware. However, most authorities place these wares amongst the earthenwares. See *English Pottery*, Griselda Lewis, Antique Collectors' Club, 1987, page 180. The jug is crisply moulded and thinly potted with figures of 'Peace' and 'Plenty', the details picked out in lime green and deep blue.
£250–£300

JOHN RIDGWAY 1815-1820
6¼ins: 16cm Unmarked.
A good quality jug, as is usual with Ridgway's products at this date. The reliefs used by the various
Staffordshire factories are much more inventive and typical of their period than are the jasper reliefs of
Wedgwood.
£250–£300

SAMUEL ALCOCK & Co. c.1845
Height 14½ins: 37cm Printed initials.
A large bone china ewer from a bedroom washing set. Samuel Alcock made a number of classically-influenced wares in the 1840s and 1850s, not only in bone china, but also in stoneware and earthenware. The colours here are a typical royal-blue ground and transfer-printed black outline coloured in peach and orange. One of the problems that this class of ware displays is visible in the photograph – the ground colour is too thin and soft and it wears badly. The bone china pieces give the curious impression of having been made in the wrong material – they should have been in earthenware.
£150–£200

WILLIAM BROWNFIELD post-1871
Height 7¼ins: 18.4cm Elaborate moulded mark and PODR.
A crisply moulded Parian jug originally issued in stoneware to commemorate the marriage of Albert Edward, Prince of Wales, later Edward VII, to Princess Alexandra of Denmark. It ranks amongst the best of the moulded jugs and remained popular under its name 'Albion' long after the wedding. This example could not have been produced before 1871, when the factory started making porcelain. It may have been designed by W.Harry Rogers. A stoneware example would be about the same price.
£100–£200

CAUGHLEY/COALPORT c.1800
Height 8¾ins: 22.3cm No mark.
A rare pair of cabbage-moulded jugs with good flower painting and a gilt JH in a wreath and gilt mask spouts. The Caughley factory sold out to Coalport in 1799.
£1200–£1800

COALPORT c.1835
Height 11½ins: 29.5cm No mark.
A well moulded and brightly enamelled bone china ewer which originally had a matching bowl forming a bedroom washing set. Now desirable for interior decoration or dried flowers. The matching basin would raise the price to £800–£1200.
£400–£600

RIDGWAY c.1815-1820
5½ins: 14cm Unmarked.
An attractive jug with white relief classical subjects against a duck-egg blue ground and with gilt details. The colour has 'crawled' in places in the firing where it did not take well to the hard body.
£180–£250

SPODE c.1835
3⅛ins: 8cm Unmarked.
An attractive bone china mug enamelled with well-painted roses. Such mugs were made in large numbers in the 19th century for christenings, marriages and various presentations such as to retiring workers. Most are inscribed in gilding and some are dated, adding to the value. They are very rarely marked. Many suffered from brownish discolorations, common to bone china of the first half of the 19th century.
£250–£350

ROYAL WORCESTER 1888
Height 5ins: 12.7cm Printed marks including registration number 29115 and date code.
A well painted and decorated jug, the flowers in botanical style and with the matt, deep colours overlaid
by a gilt transfer. Such pieces are not uncommon but have a ready market.
£80–£120

COPELAND 1860-1880
14½ins: 37cm Printed mark.
An attractive pair of ewers painted with a riot of summer flowers, possibly by C. F. Hürten. The foot and neck are turquoise and with gilt details. This pair had body cracks and a chip £800–£1200. Perfect, £1200–£1800.

DERBY c.1800
5⅛ins: 13cm Painted crown, crossed batons and D in red; titled.
A jug painted with a named view in Cumberland, the rest of the body with gilt scrollwork. Unlike most gilding on pieces of this size, it is still adhering.
£600–£900

DOULTON 1897
Height 6¾ins: 17.2cm Printed green rosette mark.
A good quality Diamond Jubilee tyg made additionally interesting, but no more valuable, by the inscription on one side recording its presentation to J.C. Bailey by Sir Henry Doulton. Bailey had suggested that Doulton introduce bone china at the Nile Street works in Burslem. Sir Henry was initially opposed but then relented, their products having huge success at the 1889 Chicago Exhibition. This tyg was probably by way of a 'thank you'.
£300–£400

UNATTRIBUTED possibly Welsh
6¼ins: 16cm Unmarked.
A bone china jug lacking a sense of direction. The body is bat-printed in black with an uncommon sea-shore scene below lightly moulded flowers which have been inexpertly hand coloured. Borders are in blue enamel. Despite the conflict between the minute detail of the scene and the giant flowers, the jug has a certain charm. £600–£800

MINTON 1840-1850
Height 9¾ins: 24.5cm No mark.
Described in the Minton shape book as a 'Sèvres Ewer', which it copies fairly faithfully (*pot à eau a la Romaine à ornements* in the Sèvres records), even to the size. The quality is high but, for modern taste, the gilding scarcely relieves the white body, making it a difficult seller.
£150–£250

PARAGON 1937(6)
Height 9½ins: 24cm Elaborate gilt mark including name.
A well-printed chromo-lithographic transfer commemorating the non-event of the Coronation of Edward VIII. This is a limited edition of five hundred, numbered on the base and in a fitted box. Most commemorative wares since 1902 were issued in vast numbers, often given to school children as souvenirs along with a one day holiday. These were cherished by their owners and have entered family folklore, usually on the theme that only three were made: one in a museum, one in America and theirs. The truth is that none are very rare and the unlimited ones rarely fetch more than £10. The fact that Edward VIII was not crowned is irrelevant. He was a very popular Prince of Wales and coronation wares are issued *in advance* of the event. In fact Edward VIII mugs are more common than those of his brother George VI as less time was available before the coronation in 1937.
£150–£250

ROCKINGHAM 1830-1842
Height 6½ins: 16.5cm Printed griffin in puce.
The handle of this mug is in the unusual form of a horse's hoof and the upper part of a horse's tail, unique to Rockingham and making it possible to differentiate unmarked mugs from similar Derby examples. The mug is extremely rare and well painted with a portrait of the Duke of Wellington in a gilt panel on a claret ground. An unmarked mug with flowers might be as little as £150–£200.
£3000–£4000

ROYAL WORCESTER 1881
Height 9¼ins: 23.5cm Printed crowned circle, date code.
Royal Worcester at its bizarre best. This rose-water sprinkler, vaguely Persian-influenced, is painted with squirrels and birds on a gilt ground. Despite their quality, the public finds these off-beat, oriental-inspired wares less easy to appreciate than Stinton cattle and they fetch less than they deserve.
£400–£600

ROYAL WORCESTER 1887
Height 9¼ins: 23.5cm Printed crowned circle, date code.
The dragon handle on this ewer is loosely based on the chilong that crawls round the shoulders of Chinese Canton-decorated vases of the mid-19th century. This is not a successful pot; the gilding is heavy-handed and the leaves are a drab brown.
£200–£300

ROYAL WORCESTER 1889
Height 8ins: 20.2cm Printed crowned circle, date code.
A neatly and attractively painted pair of ewers with named views of the Rhine and the Black Mountains NA, framed by gilt leaves. The upper handle terminal is in the form of a dolphinesque bird's head. Touches like this add to the desirability of what could have been a simple loop handle. However, the complexity and strength of the modelling is ill at ease with the delicate painting.
£1000–£1500

ROYAL WORCESTER 1890
Height 9¼ins: 23.5cm Printed crowned circle, date code and PODR
A very ugly jug based on a section of elephant tusk and given an ivory ground. The painting is of an epiphyllum, *the* flower of the 1880s and 1890s, rivalling the aspidistra (although that never got on to pots). Moore Brothers specialised in it, see page 268.
£120–£180

ROYAL WORCESTER 1892
Height 17½ins: 44.5cm Printed crowned circle, date code.
A large and decorative ewer of Persian inspiration in an ivory-coloured body with pale whip-lash floral enamelling. The neck and cover are pierced and the spout is removable. As so often with Victorian ceramics, the decoration and form do not complement one another, but are in conflict. This ewer would have been far more successful without the painting. £800–£1200

ROYAL WORCESTER 1894
Heights 5ins. and 7ins: 12.8cm and 17.7cm, date code.
Typical of numerous jugs and ewers produced by the factory in the last quarter of the 19th century, the forms continuing well into the 20th. The floral decoration is coloured and printed in gilding on to the apricot, shading to yellow, body. Pieces of Royal Worcester of this type are now popular. They are attractive and they conform in decoration – all being on similar grounds. The dates are readily decipherable and there is a good spread of common to rare, as well as a range of sizes. In addition, forgeries are almost unknown, see page 299.
£100–£200

ROYAL WORCESTER 1902

Height 9½ins: 24cm Printed crowned circle, date code.

A small ewer with fine landscape painting by Harry Davis, signed. The rest of the body is in a clear apple green. Harry Davis was arguably the best painter at Worcester at the turn of the century and would stand comparison with many pieces of the Barr, Flight and Barr period. Indeed, the form with its applied beads is also harking back to the early 19th century. We will never see the like of these again – the cost of employing artists as skilled as this would make the pieces prohibitively expensive. £1000–£1500

ROYAL WORCESTER 1907

Height 8½ins: 21.5cm Printed crowned circle, date code.

A well cast ewer with bronzed borders and a scene of sheep by Harry Davis, signed. Davis was rightly renowned for his sheep, which fetch high prices. His works are more inventive than those of the Stintons, who were quite happy to repeat the same formulae on numerous examples.
£800–£1200

ROYAL WORCESTER 1915
Height 12¼ins: 31.1cm Printed crowned circle, date code.
A pair of somewhat over-elaborate ewers, the pierced spouts making them obviously impractical. The paintings are by John Stinton, signed, and are of the usual Highland cattle. There were numerous Stintons at Worcester through the 19th and 20th centuries with varying degrees of skill. Their cattle are always knee-deep in heather in a misty Highland landscape. Apparently, the Stintons never visited Scotland, their bovine experience being drawn solely from picture postcards.
£1500–£2000

UNATTRIBUTED c.1830
Height 4ins: 10.1cm No mark.
A bone china mug of no great pretensions, but attractively painted with pink cabbage roses of the type fondly attributed to William Billingsley. The leaves and handle are gilt.
£100–£150

UNATTRIBUTED c.1840
Height 13ins: 33cm No mark.
An attractive ewer, well printed and painted with flowers and a
good decorator's piece. Originally made with a matching basin for
use as a washing set in bedrooms before plumbing. In the first half of
the 19th century these sets were of a high standard for use by the
ladies and gentlemen of the household and their guests. Generally,
in the second half of the century the gentry were 'on tap' and only
poor quality earthenware sets were made for the servants in their
garret rooms. A bowl would double the price, but on its own the
bowl would be worth only half the price of the ewer as it is less
decorative. £400–£600

UNATTRIBUTED mid-19th century
Height 6¾ins: 17cm No mark.
A large and decorative tankard, transfer-printed with a puce outline
and brightly-enamelled hand colouring. The pattern is an amusing
variation of the 18th century quail pattern, itself based on Chinese
famille-rose export pieces. The cell diaper at the mouth derives from
the same source. £250–£350

UNATTRIBUTED 1851
Height 6¾ins: 17cm Printed name and PODR.
An unusual jug with a black transfer print of the 1851 Exhibition
buildings. Although commonly referred to as the Crystal Palace,
this was the name given it by *Punch*. Apart from pot-lids, few
ceramic souvenir wares of the various International Exhibitions
were made or have survived. This jug gives the impression of its
print having been engraved for something else and applied to this
jug as an after-thought. The base mark, *J.Green*, is that of a London
retailer. £400–£600

MISCELLANEOUS

Victorian inventiveness was demonstrated not only by changes in technology, but also in the new forms in which ceramic objects were made. The vastly increased numbers of the middle classes were offered a tempting range of objects by the porcelain manufacturers, some of which had appeared in the 18th century such as inkstands and candlesticks but which were now given a 19th century twist, King John's inkwell, page 99 for example, others of which were newly designed. Here are objects that do not fit happily into other sections: whistles, egg stands and curtain 'ties', door plates and menu boards. By their very nature the objects in this section do not cohere and each object would depend on factory, quality and decorative value for its saleability.

BELLEEK c.1870
7ins: 18cm.
A scent bottle moulded and picked out in enamels with national emblems and the Star of David. These scent bottles are not uncommon and are popular with collectors. They are not marked as the Belleek's complex mark would be difficult to house without marring the design. This is well-known and does not reduce the price.
£400–£600

BELLEEK c.1870
Height 13¼ins: 33.5cm Early crest and name.
An early and rare candlestick with the boy in matt and the rest with a shiny glaze, all well modelled. The sea-urchins, here forming sconces, can be found as teapots and sugar bowls.
£700–£1000

BELLEEK c.1895
Length 16¼ins: 41.3cm Printed symbol and name.
A well-decorated mirror frame, basket-weave moulded and applied with hand-formed sprays of lily of the valley, their leaves green. The flowers and leaves are very prone to damage and are extremely difficult to restore as the nacreous glaze is almost impossible to simulate. Many frames are unmarked, and despite the fact that they could be by no other factory, the price falls by about one third. A First Period example (before 1891) would fetch £1500–£2000.
£1000–£1500

CHAMBERLAIN & Co. c.1840-1845
Length 7½ins: 19cm Printed name and history.
A model of King John's tomb in Worcester Cathedral. The exterior is brightly enamelled and gilt and the top is removable to reveal three inkwells and a pen tray. Without the wells which are frequently missing £300–£400. It was also issued in white and in stone colour. The coloured example cost £4 4s 0d in 1843, when the equivalent spending power was about £300, not a great deal different to today's value.
£500–£700

CHAMBERLAIN & Co. c.1841
Width 12ins: 30.5cm Printed name.
An extremely elaborate card tray with a well modelled and coloured border of shells and a superb scene of the (then) proposed Houses of Parliament which were started in 1840 and finished in 1852. This tray is recorded in the Chamberlain account books in July 1841: '1 shell tray, view Houses of Parliament, £5 5s 0d.' Although fussy in conception, the quality of this piece overrides any lingering condemnation of 'Victoriana', still common in the mid-1970s, when the first edition of this book appeared.
£1000–£1500

COALPORT, JOHN ROSE c.1805
10¼ins: 26cm Unmarked.
A fine pair of ice pails, covers and liners in the Regency Imari style and palette. These are very much interior decorators' taste. The fact that there is a matching dessert set in Buckingham Palace would be a strong selling point.
£4000–£6000

COALPORT c.1820
8ins: 20cm diameter.
A rarity complete, this eggstand is boldly decorated in underglaze-blue, iron-red, green and gilding. Collectors specialising in a particular factory will push up the prices of even unattractive objects if they are rare enough.
£500–£700

DERBY (attributed) c.1800
1¾ins: 4.5cm.
A bone china dog whistle, carefully painted in black and brown and with pink mouth and collar.
£250–£300

101

ROYAL CROWN DERBY 1885

Diameter 17ins: 43.5cm Printed crowned monogram, date code.

A very large and uncommon revolving waiter or 'Lazy Susan' with an Imari pattern. Not only desirable from the point of view of a Derby collector, but also a good quality and usable object. They were usually bought with a matching tea or coffee service.
£400–£600

GRAINGER & Co. 1892

Diameter 6⅛ins: 15.5cm Printed shield, date code.

A good box and cover, double-walled and pierced with scrolling picked out in gilding, the rim with turquoise beads. The design on these Grainger wares was part of the mould, the piercing being carried out by hand when the clay was leather hard. Lacking George Owen's skills at Royal Worcester, Grainger's adopted a semi-mechanical approach which was, in many ways, more inventive than Owen's repetitive holes. The slightly domed covers on these boxes are easily damaged, making perfect examples uncommon. The matt texture of the porcelain is easily imitated by a skilled restorer.
£300–£500

GRAINGER & Co. c.1900
Diameter 4½ins: 11cm Printed shield.
A box and cover with a blurry painting of a pheasant by James Stinton, the scroll-work gilt on an ivory and pink ground. It is surprising that many dealers, and presumably collectors also, since they must buy from them, fail to discriminate between good and poor examples of the Stintons' variable work. The magic of the name seems to be enough to sell the piece without objective criticism of the quality.
£250–£300

MINTON c.1830
Diameter 10ins: 25.4cm No mark.
An amazing piece of porcelain floral artistry, here surviving in good condition which is rare, considering the fragility of the petals. The whole is brightly and carefully coloured. Although unmarked, the shape is known from the factory design books and, like so much flower-encrusted ware, would at one time have been attributed to Rockingham. A true interior designer's piece which would come to life on a mahogany or rosewood table. Bad damage on a piece like this would result in a huge fall in price.
£1500–£2000

ROCKINGHAM 1826-1830
Diameter 4ins: 10.7cm Griffin in red and C1 3.
A shallow pin tray with moulded rim and a deep-blue border relieved by gilt leaf meander enclosing a naturalistic spray of flowers. This is not Rockingham on a good day. The flower spray is pedestrian and not helped by the heavy border. The black pitting in the glaze, which is not uncommon on Rockingham, is disfiguring.
£200–£300

ROCKINGHAM 1826-1830
Height 1⅞ins: 4.8cm: width 3¼ins: 8.2cm Griffin in red.
A shell-shaped inkwell moulded in the form of a scallop with two shell feet and two shell penholders. The top is painted with gilt scrolls and foliage. Complete it has an inkpot and cover £300–£500.
£200–£300

SPODE c.1830
4ins: 10.2cm Painted name and pattern number 1166.
This attractive little chamberstick is decorated with the popular sprigs of flowers against a gold-scaled,
deep blue ground.
£400–£600

SWANSEA 1814-1822
4ins: 10cm Red stencilled mark.
A stylish and attractive conceit, the bold gilt lines of the shell enclosing a band of
coloured flowers on the lid. Unusually for inkwells, this has not only its lid, but also
the original liner. This was restored and the body had a hair crack £250–£300. A
perfect example would be £500–£600.

WEDGWOOD 1920s
Diameter 2ins: 5.1cm Printed vase and name.
A rare Fairyland brooch with a polychrome and
gilt pixie against a mottled beige ground. A
similar sized brooch with a butterfly would be
£100. The mounts are of little consequence
unless in gold; an unmounted example would
fetch the same as one in gilt metal. £600–£800

W. H. GOSS c.1900
3ins: 7.6cm Printed mark.
William Henry Goss' brilliant idea was to ensure that every visitor, particularly cyclists (visiting famous landmarks was all the rage on the new Safety bicycles), had a souvenir to take home. The little pots with coats of arms of the area can be found from about £10 a time, the 'cottages' (which include town crosses, large houses and so on) are rarer. The record stands at over £1000. This is a 16th century courthouse in Christchurch, Hampshire. £300–£500

HAMMERSLEY & Co. c.1890

Candlesticks 6½ins: 16.5cm Printed marks in green including patent number 3872.

A bone china dressing-table set painted with bold roses and gilding. The thinly cast forms are borrowed loosely from 18th century Meissen, probably via contemporary Dresden or Thuringian pieces. Hammersley was by no means one of the major factories of the period but some designs, such as this, are competent and very decorative. Like any decorative object of reasonable quality, they have risen considerably in the last few years. £250–£300

WORCESTER, FLIGHT, BARR and BARR c. 1825

Diameter 9ins: 23cm Printed name.

A card tray with overhead handle springing from gilt leaves on the lime-green ground. The central panel with a scene from the popular novel, *Paul and Virginia*, which was published in 1787. Adapted as a play, it was performed to huge acclaim by Madame Vestris at Drury Lane in 1822. It was probably this production that prompted the tray. Subjects from the story are frequently found on English ceramics including pot-lids and Staffordshire figures, as well as on Continental pieces. Trays with overhead handles are rarely found intact. Often the handle has 'sprung' and a single crack has appeared spontaneously. It is unwise to pick up *any* ceramic object by the handle. £600–£900

WORCESTER, BARR, FLIGHT and BARR 1807-1813

Length 6ins: 15.3cm Painted name etc.

An attractive ingot-shaped inkstand, well painted with panels of summer flowers. The ends with gilt lyres and scrolls on a deep-blue ground, the handle in the form of twisted dolphin. This example lacks one of the two inkwells. A complete example £500–£700. £350–£500

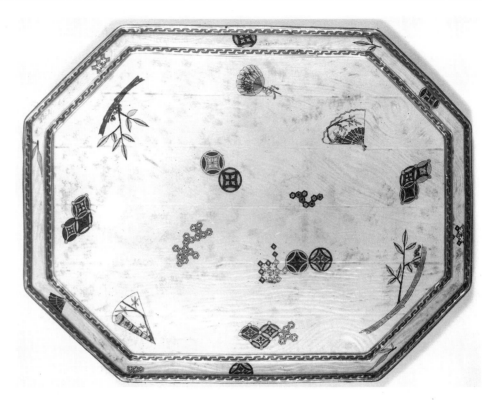

ROYAL WORCESTER c. 1875
Length 17ins: 43cm Impressed crowned circle.
A Japanese influenced tray with bright enamels
on a simulated wood grain. Originally made for a
tea service which would fetch £600–£800
complete. The small designs float in too empty a
space to be effective.
£200–£300

ROYAL WORCESTER 1880
*Height 13¼ins: 34 cm Printed crowned circle, date
code.*
A bizarre and very rare candlestick in the form
of a Japanese juggler, the colours in warm tones
of bronze, dark brown and gilding on an ivory
body. Of all split pairs of objects, candlesticks
suffer the greatest fall in price. In many cases a
pair of objects will be worth three times the
price of a single; with candlesticks four times is
more likely.
£600–£900

ROYAL WORCESTER 1897
Height 5¾ins: 14.7cm Printed crowned circle, date code.
An amusing menu card simulating a battered fence on a tree stump. The 'Wild West' conception is feminised by the incongruous apricot, peach and gilt coloration. Worcester produced numerous forms of name and menu card holders which would all fetch around the same price. Set of a usable eight £700–£1000.
£70–£100

ROYAL WORCESTER 1887
Height 8ins: 20cm Crowned circle, date code.
Candlesticks are uncommon from Royal Worcester, but also not very attractive or collectable. While this example is unusual and well made in peach with gilt details, the elements of the design are poorly related. Pair: £300–£500.
£120–£180

POSSIBLY CHAMBERLAIN'S, WORCESTER c.1800-1810.
Height 8⅝ins: 22cm No mark.
A pair of bough pots lacking their covers. While they look acceptable photographed from almost straight on, viewed from above, a more likely angle, the gaping white hole is all too obvious. Buying from a catalogue without careful thought can be a pitfall. A lid of pierced distressed painted tin plate could be the solution or they could simply be filled with pot-pourri. They are well painted with displays of fruit and foliage and are very decorative.
£1500–£2000

DERBY c.1800
Height 8¾ins: 22cm Crowned D, incised 76, crossed batons and title.
A bough pot and cover painted, probably by John Brewer, with a view of 'near Malvern, Worcestershire'. There were two Brewers, John and Robert, and making attributions to them or, indeed, other painters at the factory, is speculative. We may never know, and 'in the style of...' is probably the best one can do.
£1500–£2000

COPELAND & GARRETT c.1840
Height 5¾ins: 14.7cm Printed green wreath mark.
A very rare curtain tie-back. The domed disc is moulded with scrolls and painted and gilt, enclosing a superbly painted arrangement of summer flowers probably by David Evans. The back has an integral boss inset with a screw-threaded brass nut set in plaster. Copeland and Garrett are the last of the great 'undiscovered' factories of the 19th century and there is no monograph on the factory.
£400–£600

ROYAL WORCESTER 1901
Length 10ins: 25.5cm Printed crowned circle, date code.
A few years ago cheese dishes were almost unsaleable, but they have recently developed a strong following. This example is not particularly well decorated and has worn gilding. Better example £300–£400.
£150–£250

ROYAL WORCESTER 1906
Diameter 3¼ins: 8.2cm Printed crowned circle, date code.
A badly moulded posy-holder in white with a sage-green lily-leaf base. The overall effect is dull, if not sinister, making this an undesirable and cheap object.
£60–£80

ROYAL WORCESTER 1921
Diameter 7¼ins: 18.5cm Printed crowned circle, date code.
A late piece with printed outlines coloured and gilt on a peach ground. The spikes of the shell are obviously damage-prone and the small shell feet can become detached.
£150–£250

ROYAL WORCESTER 1930s
Height 3ins: 7.5cm Printed crowned circle, date code.
A miniature Toby jug, loosely based on an 18th century, but larger, original and made in a number of sizes up to 6ins: 5.2cm.
£80–£120

ROYAL WORCESTER 1974
Height 4ins: 10cm Printed crowned circle, date code.
A candle snuffer in the form of a nun, companion to a monk. Both were made in the 1860s and continue in production today, the earlier examples up to £120–£180. Rarer forms can make over £1000. £60–£100

STAFFORDSHIRE c.1820
7¼ins: 18.3cm Unmarked.
A large and good fox-head stirrup cup. Many examples have collars, often inscribed in gilding (as this one is) 'TALLY-HO'. The stirrup cup, filled with something alcoholic and warming, was handed to the huntsman before setting off and was drained before setting down. They were popular in the first half of the century and were made in both pottery and porcelain. This example was exceptional, others, less good, will sell for £300 upwards. £800–£1200

PROBABLY ROBINSON AND LEADBEATER mid-19th century
6ins: 15.2cm.
An uncommon tinted Parian trinket box and cover. Sleeping children were a popular subject in Victorian times when sentimentality was rampant. Oddly, the classes which could afford works of art handed their children over to nannies who brought them up. The parents saw them only just before bedtime or on Sundays; this box, sitting on a lady's dressing table, may have reminded her of what she was missing.
£150–£250

UNATTRIBUTED c.1825
Height 8½ins: 21.5cm No mark.
A watch-holder in the form of a church tower, unusually sharply modelled and well painted and applied with flowers. The green base is gilt-lined. Tower watch-stands are also known in Staffordshire pottery and were used to hold the owner's gold fob-watch when he retired for the night. The demand for gothicky ruins and obelisks is strong and a well made piece such as this would prove very saleable. It would be relatively simple and inexpensive to have the hole fitted with a quartz clock movement to convert it into a usable clock.
£600–£900

UNATTRIBUTED 1889
(hallmark) Height 2⅛ins: 5.5cm, PODR.
A silver-mounted scent bottle, datable from the mount. Not an identifiable factory, although at first glance it looks like Derby. Small scent bottles are a popular collecting field with examples appearing in ceramics, silver and glass.
£150–£200

UNATTRIBUTED c.1840
Height 11½ins: 29.2cm No mark.
Although very well painted and gilt, this door plate would not prove very saleable. Few people would now risk screwing them to a door and they are not easy to display in a collection. Even marked examples by Coalport or Copeland & Garrett would be little more expensive.
£150–£200

PLAQUES

Slabs of pottery or porcelain were made for a variety of purposes: to roll pills on, to act as palettes for oil or watercolour painting, as wall or stove tiles and as a 'canvas' for the ceramic painter to display his skills. In many cases, the painted plaque was not a factory product, it was produced by the painter in his own time and sold on his own behalf. Most of the painters would be employed by the factory to paint tea and dinner services, vases and so on, but a few may have been outside decorators working solely on their own behalf. A few plaques were painted by amateurs in the late 19th century, although they mainly restricted themselves to plates and dishes.

Painting in oils on milk-white glass resembling porcelain was common at this date and such 'cold painted' pieces have been mistaken for fired enamels by the unwary. A minute scratch with a pin or knife will establish the medium. Plaques are rarely marked and it is dangerous to attribute them to a particular factory unless the painter can be firmly identified and his place of work is known. As ceramic painters were, particularly in the first half of the 19th century, an itinerant lot, even this is not foolproof. Where a firm attribution is possible, the price will certainly be increased, as it will if there is a signature and date. Named scenes are also better than unnamed unless the view, such as Windsor Castle, is obvious.

Amongst the most popular subjects are floral studies – the lusher the better. These have now caught up with similar paintings on canvas, having been a quarter of the price ten years ago. At the end of the 19th century and into the 20th, several factories had their painters sign their work and some specialised in plaques, particularly Royal Worcester and Aynsley.

UNATTRIBUTED c.1830
7⅛ins by 9½ins: 18cm by 24cm Unmarked.
A well-painted plaque of small size. As so often, it is unsigned and unmarked. Most would seem to have been painted by factory painters in their own time. At one time under-appreciated, flower-painted plaques have risen sharply.
£600–£900

DIXON c.1830-1860
8¾ins by 6½ins: 22.2cm by 16.5cm Impressed Dixon.
One of a pair of plaques painted with the desirable subject of parrots and parakeets. Although very saleable, the birds give the uncomfortable impression of being not only stuffed but about to topple off the branches they are perched on. In all probability they were copied from a natural history book. Plaques are rarely marked and the name Dixon is unrecorded. It may just possibly be the name of the painter who had ordered the plaques from one of the factories, several Dixons are recorded as porcelain painters.
£1000–£1500

COPELAND 1860-1870
Diameter 16ins: 41cm No mark.
A superb large plaque painted by C(harles). F(erdinand). Hürten, signed, with pink and yellow roses beside an ivy-overgrown wall. Hürten was one of the best painters of the period, making his name at the Paris Exhibition of 1858 and being hired by Copeland the following year. See also the vases on pages 247, 248. One of a set of the seasons £800–£1200.

COPELAND c.1875
Length 27¾ins: 70.5cm Impressed name.
A well-painted plaque by Lucien Besche who was, like so many Staffordshire painters of the time, French. Most were escaping from The Franco-Prussian War of 1870-71. He started at Minton's before joining Copeland in 1872. He later returned to oils and to ballet designs. His ceramic technique is akin to that of the miniature painter – a series of minute strokes to build up the design. This was usually not original but copied from a well-known master, often Boucher or Watteau. Despite the high quality of this plaque, an identical Berlin example would fetch £3000–£4000.
£1500–£2000

DERBY 1877
Diameter 15¼ins: 38.6cm No mark.
Derby plaques are rare and this example is particularly well painted by the sought-after artist, James Rouse, senior. It depicts 'The Royal Pets' after Landseer and is signed and dated 1877. Dogs are perennial favourites and the parrot lends an exotic touch.
£2000–£3000

DERBY CROWN PORCELAIN COMPANY c.1880
Height 17½ins: 44.5 cm Printed monogram.
A superbly painted plaque by G.Landgraf, signed. The background, too subtle to photograph, is in white enamel with a *bianco-sopra-bianco* damask design of leaves and berries. Landgraf worked at Brown-Westhead, Moore's factory until 1880 when he transferred to Derby, where he stayed for only three years. His work is rare, of high quality and very collectable.
£2500–£3500

MINTON 1841
4¾ins by 3½ins: 12cm by 9cm.
A good documentary plaque by John Simpson and inscribed on the reverse: *Mrs. William Keary, painted by John Simpson, Stoke upon Trent, 1841.* The quality of Simpson's work is high and fairly easy to identify, but it is the inscription that makes this plaque particularly saleable; without it £500–£800. J. Simpson was the son of a Derby painter, where he was first employed, working for Minton's from about 1837-47.
£800–£1200

MINTON(S) 1865-1885
*5ins by 8ins: 12.7cm by 20.3cm
No mark.*
A named view of Stokesay Castle painted by J.Evans, signed. John Bishop Evans worked at Minton's from about 1865 until 1885, specialising in land and seascapes.
£600–£900

MINTONS c.1885
7ins by 10ins: 17.8cm by 25.4cm No mark.
One of the subjects of which Louis Marc Solon was so enamoured – suffering putti. Here five are chained and caged around a diaphanously clad maiden, all in white pâte-sur-pâte on an olive-green slab. As is almost always the case, well executed, and with more action than usual. Solon's work fades in and out of popularity on a five year cycle, now in. Compare with the following. £4000–£6000

MINTONS 1904-1913
8¼ins by 4½ins: 21.5cm by 11.5cm
No mark.
A pâte-sur-pâte plaque by L(ouis Marc). Solon, signed at the base of the pillar, with 'The Ladder to Glory' in white on a green-blue background. The more usual form of plaque in which the background is left blank, the figures floating in space.
£2000–£3000

WEDGWOOD 1920s
Diameter 12¼ins: 31cm Printed vase and name Z4968.
A large wall plaque with a bold Fairyland design entitled *Imps on a Bridge and Tree House.* The reverse has, apart from the standard vase mark, an H in a chrysanthemum scroll.
£1500–£2000

WEDGWOOD 1920s
10¾ins by 7¾ins: 27.6cm by 21cm Printed vase and name Z5331.
A fine Wedgwood plaque named Torches incorporating the signature of Daisy Makeig-Jones, an uncommon feature. This was part of the print, not hand executed. The brilliant colours and gilding are well registered, making this amongst the most desirable of all Fairyland items.
£3000–£4000

ROYAL WORCESTER c.1870
8¼ ins by 9½ins: 20.6cm by 25cm No mark.
Painted by R(obert). F.Perling, signed, after the original by Sir Edwin Landseer. Perling was a painter at Worcester from 1855 to 1885 and produced many plaques, several after Landseer. The companion plaque is the much less desirable subject of the dying stag washed down a ravine accompanied by drowning hounds. £800–£1200

ROYAL WORCESTER 1903
10½ ins by 13¾ins: 26.7cm by 35cm No mark.
An unusually large plaque of Windsor Castle by Harry Davis, signed and dated. As is so often the case with plaques, there is no mark. Finely painted plaques and vases by Royal Worcester artists have been consistently high performers amongst 19th century porcelain.
£1500–£2000

ROYAL WORCESTER 1925

15¾ ins by 18⅞ins: 40cm by 48cm Printed crowned circle and date code.

An unusually large plaque painted by H(arry). Davis, signed, with his favourite subject. Well painted plaques have shown a marked increase in price recently.
£2000–£3000

UNATTRIBUTED 1826

6¼ ins by 5ins: 16cm by 13cm Title and date on reverse.

A charming plaque painted by William Corden with a portrait of William Rudyerd Williams-Wynn on his third birthday, and his dog, Fidelle. The dog has not only been taught to beg, but also to balance a toothsome morsel on its nose. It was common practice to dress small boys in dresses until the middle of the 19th century. Corden was apprenticed, and worked, at the Nottingham Road Works in Derby until about 1825 when he set up as a portrait painter in London.
£1000–£1500

UNATTRIBUTED c.1830
Height 4¾ins: 12cm No mark.
A fairly well painted plaque with a scene from Shakespeare's *Measure for Measure*. The technique is of small streaks or dots of colour to build up the picture, suggesting that the painter was more used to working on ivory and painting miniatures.
£400–£600

UNATTRIBUTED c.1830
9¼ins by 7½ins: 23.5cm by 19cm No mark.
Porcelain plaques are rarely marked and many were produced by painters working in their own time on bought-in blanks. Attributing them is, therefore, a notoriously risky business. This is an attractive example with well-painted flowers. While flowers have always been popular in garden-conscious Britain, flower-painted objects have taken an upward leap in price in the last few years.
£500–£700

UNATTRIBUTED First half of the 19th century
8ins by 7ins: 20.5cm by 18cm No mark.
An anonymous gentleman, an anonymous factory and an anonymous painter of small ability, make this plaque ceramically unexciting. A large number of comparable plaques by amateur-like artists (note the awkward placing of the sitter's legs) were produced in the first half of the 19th century. Some manage, at least, some charm which makes them more expensive, others a disquieting strangeness – which does not.
£300–£500

UNATTRIBUTED c.1850-1860
7¾ins by 9¾ins: 18.5cm by 24.8cm No mark.
An attractive plaque with a collection of brightly coloured flowers. It suffers from a lack of coherence and the diagonal construction is off-putting. The presence of heather in English flower painting is a fairly reliable guide to dating. Albert and Victoria leased Balmoral in 1848, later buying it, and all things Caledonian became the rage – including heather. Compare the quality of the painting with the plaque on page 118.
£300–£400

UNATTRIBUTED 1855
6¾ ins by 5¼ins: 17.5cm by 13.3cm No mark.
A portrait plaque of Marie Henriette, Duchess of Brabant, after the original by Sir William Ross, and painted by J. Simpson, signed, titled and dated 1855. The quality is high, but the subject is rather less attractive than Mrs. Keary, another subject by Simpson, page 122. It is also a copy of another artist's work, making this less desirable. After leaving Minton's in 1847 there is no definite record of Simpson at another factory, although he may have been at Copeland or Ridgway. It is also possible he became a freelance working on bought-in blanks. £600–£900

UNATTRIBUTED 1859

14½ ins by 11ins: 36.5cm by 28cm No mark.

An exceptionally fine plaque which is comparable with any from Berlin. It was painted by William B.Ford, signed and dated 1859, after the original oil by J.L.Dyckmans. Ford (1822-1896) was an enamellist on both copper and porcelain, this plaque of a blind beggar having been exhibited at the Royal Academy in 1860. Its drawback against a high price is its subject – blind beggars are not the most endearing of subjects. £2000–£2500

UNATTRIBUTED c.1870
16ins by 11¾ins: 40.5cm by 29.8cm No mark.
An anonymous but quite good plaque of a not unattractive subject.
It would be much cheaper than a comparable scene on canvas.
£800–£1200

UNATTRIBUTED c.1880
8¼ins by 10ins: 21cm by 26cm No mark.
A quite well executed plaque after a scene by the popular Victorian
artist, Birket Foster. In all probability it was copied from one of the
numerous wood engraved or colour-printed reproductions of his
work in a book of the time. Landscapes are popular subjects, as with
oil paintings, and reach higher prices than anonymous portraits,
again as with paintings. Pair £1500–£2000.
£500–£800

PLATES AND TABLEWARES

The decorative possibilities of the flat plate were recognised by the Chinese over a thousand years ago. The large blue and white dishes imported into Europe in quantities from the 16th century inspired the production of majolica, faience, Delftware and ultimately European porcelain.

In the 18th century, factories on the Continent and then in England began the manufacture of dinner services, many of which have now been broken up and single plates from the most extravagant of these can make thousands of pounds at auction. Rarely do individual 19th century plates warrant a single lot, but this is becoming increasingly common. The dedicated collectors of Swansea, Nantgarw, Rockingham and other early 19th century factories are now willing to spend several thousand pounds on the better single plates.

At the other end of the scale it is still possible to buy odd plates with a transfer-printed design from the late 19th century for a pound or two. Transfer-printing, a technique developed in the 18th century to speed up production, remained an almost exclusively British prerogative. It could be used in cobalt blue under the glaze or other colours over the glaze, often serving as a guide for hand enamelling. A variant was bat-printing, which had its heyday in the early years of the 19th century. The Wedgwood Fairyland subjects were a clever mixture of printing and hand-colouring. An outline print on the object served as a guide for the hand-colouring, which was then fired. A second pull was taken from the same printing plate, this time in gold, and superimposed over the original lines, hiding them and tying the whole lot together.

It was extremely rare for plates to be signed by their painters in the 18th century or in the first half of the 19th, but examples do exist and are the subject of strong competition when they appear on the market. The practice increased slowly over the years and by 1880 was not uncommon in the major factories such as Royal Worcester, Minton and Derby. From about the same time, painting on porcelain and pottery by amateurs became all the rage. Blanks were bought from manufacturers and these were uncommonly marked. The 'artist' then painted the design, often copied from a popular painting of the day, and frequently signed it and dated it, usually in very large letters. Such pieces sell as decoration, the price being dictated by how well it was done and the subject. From the turn of the 18th/19th century, it was common practice to identify flowers by naming them on the underside, this adds to the interest and value.

Dessert, which in the 18th and 19th centuries meant fruit, was eaten from the richest possible plates. They rarely matched the dinner service. Centuries old dinner services can still be used but dessert as a course has vanished. Most dessert services are displayed in cabinets or the sets have been broken for pairs or sale as singles. As price rise, more and more sets will be split as the collector becomes less able to afford them. Eventually, perhaps thirty years from now, the market will wake up to what is happening and the practice will stop, just as it has with sets of maps in atlases. A typical dessert set of the early 19th century comprised eighteen plates, six shaped dishes of different form (usually two square, two shell-shaped and two lozenge) and a stand. This format gave way to the Victorian dessert set of the same number of plates, plus four low and one high tazza. There were, however, variations. As today, one could order however many plates and other pieces one liked from the retailer. There is, therefore, no such thing as a 'complete' service.

BELLEEK c.1870
Height 13ins: 33cm Impressed name, retailer's mark.
A pair of centrepieces from a service, identical to one ordered for Albert Edward, Prince of Wales, later Edward VII. It has become known as the Prince of Wales service, but does this not mean that examples are escapees from the Royal Collection. As usual, they are palely-tinted and nacreous-glazed. Prices for major pieces of Belleek such as these have strengthened considerably in the last few years.
£600–£800 each

BROWN, WESTHEAD, MOORE and Co. 1868
Plates 9ins: 23cm Pattern no. B 4342 and PODR.
Part of a dessert service, each piece printed and painted with flowers on a lime green ground. A somewhat uninspiring service with too much white showing to be either a breaker or for display. It would be, however, ideal for use. Odd plates £20.

CAULDON c.1900
Diameter 8½ins: 21.7cm Printed name, retailer's name.
One of a set of sixteen bone china game plates in a fitted box, each well painted with a different named bird or beast by J. Birbeck, signed. The royal blue rim with relief gilt scrollwork. Cauldon is not noted for such a high standard of production and there is no strong demand from collectors. However, a set of this quality transcends factory collecting and stands on its own merits.
£100 each

CHAMBERLAIN WORCESTER c.1816
8¼ins: 21cm Printed crown and wreath and New Bond Street address.
An attractive dessert dish, well-painted with flowers and with a pale blue ground. A pair would be three times the price.
£200–£300

CHAMBERLAIN c.1820
Diameter 8ins: 20.2cm Painted name.
A superb plate, probably painted by Thomas Baxter, on the highly translucent 'Regent China' body. A companion plate is illustrated in *Chamberlain Worcester Porcelain* col. pl. XVIII and Godden suggests that it may be identified as from a set of thirty supplied to John Eversley in 1820 at a cost of £2 17s. 6d each. Any such pedigree and illustration in a standard monograph will enormously help the price.
£1000–£1500

Probably SAMUEL ALCOCK mid-19th century
Approx. 8ins: 20.2cm Pattern No. 3/3327.
A dessert plate well painted with a poppy from a service, each with a botanical specimen named on the
reverse. There is no factory mark, but the pattern number with a '3' above suggests a large production,
with Ridgway or Samuel Alcock as most likely candidates. However, the '3' above was used by Ridgway
on cabinet objects leaving Alcock, a factory deserving greater recognition, as the front runner.
£60–£90

COALPORT c.1810
22ins: 56cm overall Unmarked.
A rare complete supper set with its original brass-handled wooden tray. Such sets are uncommon complete and even this one has a hair crack and chip. Unlike a soup tureen, for example, they are slightly uncomfortable as decoration. £1200–£1800

COALPORT 1808 and 1809
Diameter 9½ins: 24cm No mark.
A pair of extraordinarily rare plates, one of only a few known, which are painted by Thomas Baxter in London on Coalport blanks and signed and dated by him. As can be seen on the photograph, there is some wear to the wide band of burnished gold, reducing the price from £4000. Another pair is in the Victoria & Albert Museum and is illustrated in *Coalport and Coalbrookdale*, pl.92. £2000–£3000

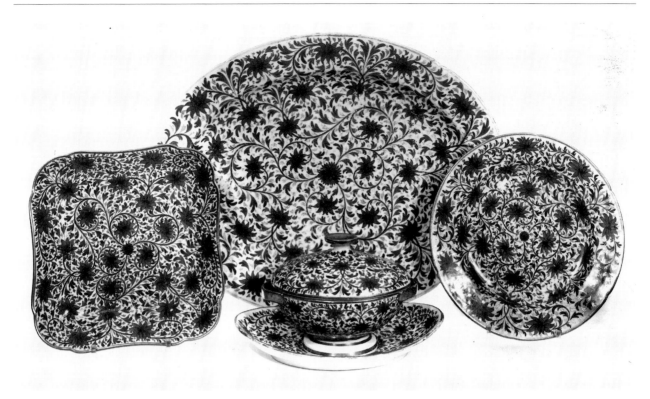

COALPORT? c.1825
No mark.
A brightly-decorated service, each piece painted with iron-red and gilt chrysanthemums. Sets of this date in usable quantities are rarely met with today and would certainly be split if encountered. The design and colouring are so overpowering it is difficult to image what one could eat off them. Pair of tureens covers and stands £500–£700, pair of plates £200–£300, large meat dish £250–£300, soup tureen £400–£600.

COALPORT c.1830
No mark.
Samples from a fine fruit service, each piece with a different landscape scene populated with figures, always a plus point. Pair of sauce tureens, covers and stands £1500–£2000, plates £600–£800, dishes £700–£1000. A similar set has the variation of the National emblems on the border. The Coalport paste at this date transmits a pure white with considerable translucency, akin to Swansea with which it can be confused.

JOHN ROSE, COALPORT c.1815-1825
Plates 9⅜ins: 24 cm Red printed 'Feltspar Porcelain' and name, impressed numeral.
A fine botanical dessert service with well-painted flowers, within a pale blue border with low relief white flowers. The 'Feltspar' refers to this particular body which contained feldspar. It was also used by Spode, who spelled it 'felspar'. A pair of plates £400–£600, a pair of dishes £700–£1000.

H & R DANIEL c.1835

7¾ins: 19.8cm Unmarked.

An eccentric bone china dessert dish painted with an exotic bird on a skeleton leaf and butterflies similarly posed. The decoration has been taken from contemporary Chinese leaf paintings and the artist has painted in every vein, an absurdly arduous task. Daniel is a highly sought after factory and pieces make very high prices. The original leaf paintings cost about £15-£20 each.

£400–£600

141

COALPORT c.1850
Diameter 9½ins: 24cm Printed name.
A well painted and gilt dessert plate with panels of flowers on a pink border, owing its origins to Sèvres in about 1760. Pink, (*rose* at Sèvres) was a popular colour in the 19th century when the French factory was in strong demand from collectors. A set of twelve with four low and a high tazza £3000–£4000.

COALPORT c.1860
No mark.
Samples from a dessert service, each painted with a different fruit within gilt and coloured borders enclosing a squirrel crest. Stands at this date are liable to become detached from their feet, whatever the factory. The glaze often settles in a crackled ring at the junction of the two parts, making restoration easy to disguise. Stands £200–£400, plates £100–£150.

COALPORT 1861-1865
Length 17¼ins: 43.5cm Painted name.
This tray has a deep red and gilt border enclosing a grey monochrome painting of figures symbolic of 'Sleep and Death bearing Sarpedon' by Robert Frederick Abraham. Abraham (1827-1895) worked at Coalport as the 'principal painter of the day', according to the *Art Journal*, until leaving to become Art Director at Copelands. This dish would fetch considerably more with a less mournful subject.
£800–£1200

DERBY c. 1800
8¾ins: 22.2cm Red crown over batons, dots and D.
An Imari-style dessert plate which could have been made by many factories, although Derby was the most prolific. Derby plates at this date are often heavily potted, finely crazed and may be discoloured. The Imari patterns are bright and bold but *en masse* can be overpowering. Similarly, individual plates will swamp more delicately painted floral subjects and Imari patterns of the first quarter of the 19th century represent good value.
£80–£120

MINTONS 1880
11½ins: 29.2cm Printed gilt globe mark, impressed name and date code.
A tazza and cover of uncommon shape and well decorated in pâte-sur-pâte with white scrolls, trophies
and putti as herms. It sold for £330 in1972. It is unsigned but is probably by Alboin Birks, as the non-
violence being doled out to the putti and the lack of signature suggests that it is not by Solon.
£1000–£1500

COPELAND mid-19th century (after 1847)
Diameter 9ins: 23cm Printed name.
The gilt scroll border here encloses a band of well-painted, bright summer flowers. The difference in price between a plate with a fully painted centre and one which is all white or with a single sprig is great. A large spray in the centre would more than double the price.
£100–£150

COPELAND & GARRETT mid-19th century (before 1847)
Diameter 9ins: 23cm Printed name.
The same shape plate as above and not untypical of thousands of odd plates left over from services and now lurking unloved in antique shops all over the country. The wavy ribbon is a favourite motif of the 1840s to 1860s. The flowers are hand coloured over a puce outline against a lime-green ground. This example is worn, making it almost valueless, a perfect one would fetch £30.
£10–£20

DAVENPORT c.1805-1815
Overall length 11¼ins: 28.5cm Longport in red script.
A pierced dessert basket painted with a Chinese garden scene in colourful enamels between gilt twig
handles. Davenport is just beginning to gain the reputation it deserves as one of the better Staffordshire
factories. Early Davenport with the 'Longport' mark is uncommon.
£300–£500

DAVENPORT 1830-1837 (c.1835)
No mark.
A fine botanically decorated service, each with a different flower within scroll borders in blue and
gilding. A full service would comprise a fruit stand (£300–£500), two sauce tureens, covers and stands
(£500–£800), four oval dishes (£500–£800), four rectangular dishes (£500–£800 a pair) and twenty-four
plates (£300–£500 a pair). If the flowers were named on the reverse the price would rise by about 20%.

NANTGARW c.1814-1823
9¾ins: 24.75cm Impressed NANT-GARW / C.W.
A rare London decorated plate imitating closely a Meissen original painted by Johann Georg Heintze in the 1740s. Several Nantgarw examples are known and they may well have been made as replacements to a Meissen set. Because they are not original conceptions, replacements are often unpopular with collectors. Almost any other comparable quality Nantgarw plate would make considerably more.
£1500–£2000

SPODE c.1805
Length 11¼ins: 28.5cm Red painted Spode and pattern number 2027.
A fine quality dish from a dessert service with moulded flowers reserved white on a pale blue ground and with well-painted floral sprays and gilding. Plates and dishes of this standard of decorativeness are strongly in demand.
£200–£300

DAVENPORT c.1845-1855
Dish 16½ins: 42cm Printed name.
A tureen, cover and stand and a meat dish from a dinner service, each well painted with sprays of flowers within a gilt border. A large service of this pattern could sell either for use, for display or be split. If each piece was marked, the latter is the most likely. Meat dish £300, tureen £250–£300, plate £80.

DAVENPORT 1856
Diameter 9¾ins: 24.8cm Printed name PODR.
An attractive and well-painted plate from a dessert service, each with a different named fruit, the border puce and gilt. Wear on a plate of this type will dramatically affect the price. The Davenport factory at Longport produced both pottery and porcelain, mostly of a good average standard. £120–£150

DAVENPORT 1870-1886
Diameter 9½ins: 24cm Printed name.
Davenport made both very high quality porcelain in the 1840s-1860s (often unmarked) and also mass-produced wares for the lower end of the market. This continued to the end of the period but one meets fewer and fewer of the better items. Whereas dessert services from the beginning of the 19th century usually struck the right balance between the border and the flower painting, by the 1860s the former began to overpower the flowers. Generally the quality of the botanical work was also less fine. Stand £100–£150, pair of plates £100–£150.

DERBY First quarter of the 19th century
Stand 15¾ins: 40cm
Painted crossed batons and crown.
A good quality tureen and stand with an attractive design of coloured roses and garlands of cornflowers and gilt leaves corresponding to pattern number 1796. The predominance of pink in the palette makes this of strong feminine appeal, ideal for interior décor. The Derby paste in the first quarter of the 19th century during the Bloor period (1820-48) can suffer from a disfiguring crazing and staining, particularly where a piece has been chipped or cracked. £150–£200; pair of plates £80–£120.

STAFFORDSHIRE c.1830-1840

9ins: 23cm Unmarked.

The blue bordered bone china plate has a fair degree of Sèvres influence, the shells being recorded on both plates and more complex wares. The flower painting is uninspired and the various elements of the design are not well intregrated. Nevertheless, it is a decorative plate of good quality. The bone china dessert plate is typical of many dessert wares of the period with ill-defined moulding and no gilding. The flowers have a certain verve which is quite appealing. Wares of this type often have black specks due to badly refined clay and the body may craze and discolour. £40–£100 for plates of this type.

ROYAL WORCESTER c.1860-1870

Diameter 9¼ins: 23.5cm Impressed crown and circle.

A bone china plate painted by the Cantonese artist Po-Hing, who was employed by Reginald Binns and who worked at Worcester in the 1860s and 1870s. Plates are the most common but vases are also known by him. The quality of his work is comparable with Chinese decoration at Canton in the mid-19th century. Other pieces of English pottery and porcelain have come to notice with Canton figure, flower and bird subjects, probably also by the same hand.

£400–£600

DERBY c.1810
Diameter 8⅞ins: 22.5cm Painted mark.
A pair of finely painted plates, titled on the reverse 'A Wreck' and 'In Italy'. It was not uncommon for Derby and other factories to gild sets of dessert plates with differing, but complementary, borders, as here. Leaving aside the wear to the gilding of the first example, it would still fetch less than the right as shipwrecks are much less saleable than peaceful scenes. A plate, apparently from the same service, is illustrated in *Derby Porcelain*, pl.113 and attributed to the hand of George Robertson.
£1500–£2000

DERBY CROWN PORCELAIN Co. 1878
Diameter 8ins: 20.2cm Printed crowned monogram, date code.
A plate from a rich, relief-gilt dessert service with the flowers and butterflies in burnished gold and silver, touched in with enamel, all on an ivory ground. Relief gilding was popular at this date and it can hardly have been intended for these plates to be used as the silver (actually platinum) and gold would not wear well. If they have been used, the scratching reduces the price considerably.
£80–£120

153

**DERBY CROWN
PORCELAIN Co. 1884**
*Diameter approx 9ins: 24cm
Impressed and printed monogram
and crown, date code.*
An unusual plate from a dessert
service, designed by John
Joseph Brownsword who was
Principal of Hull Art School.
The transfer-printed scenes of
children at play were inspired
by the book illustrator Kate
Greenaway. The claret border
has hand-tinted flowers.
£250–£300.

**DERBY CROWN
PORCELAIN Co. 1890**
*Printed monogram, retailer's
mark and date code.*
A muffin dish and cover and a
serving dish from a service with
pastel-coloured and gilt wild
flowers, grasses and butterflies
painted by John P. Wade and
with the monogram CHS. An
attractive crest adds value to a
service, particularly if traceable
to a well-known family. Arms,
much rarer as subsidiary
decoration, are better still but
monograms are generally not
desirable. Some factories and
retailers still have records
which might enable the
original owner to be traced, but
the chances are not good. Dish
£100–£150, muffin dish
£100–£200.

DERBY c.1888
Diameter 9¼ins: 23.5cm Impressed name, printed monogram and crown.
One of a well-known series of plates painted by James Rouse, senior (1802-1888), signed on the reverse. The flowers are well painted in bright enamels. It is not recorded how many were painted, but several have appeared in the salerooms over the years. Rouse, whose work is very desirable returned to the style of flower painting akin to that of the early 19th century. He worked at Coalport from about 1827-60, at the King Street factory from about 1875-82 and at the Royal Crown Derby factory until he died.
£700–£1000

ROYAL CROWN DERBY 1893
Diameter 9ins: 22.8cm Printed crown and cypher, date code, PODR.
A very rare and finely decorated plate painted by P. Taillandier, signed, with a portrait within a candy-pink border. The rim is pierced and gilt and potted to 'eggshell' thinness. Little is known about Taillandier. A plate such as this would never have been meant for use and continues the 18th century practice of producing dessert plates for admiration, probably in a cabinet.
£500–£800

ROYAL CROWN DERBY 1913
Length 10½ins: 26.5cm Printed monogram and crown, date code.
A good quality but rather dull dessert dish, sparsely painted with flower sprays within a dark blue and gilt rim. There would have been a pair of these in the service, along with two further pairs of dishes, a tazza and the plates, probably eighteen.
£1200–£1800 the service

ROYAL CROWN DERBY 1946
Diameter 10ins: 25.4cm Impressed and printed monogram, crown, date code.
An interesting commemorative plate for the 1946 Cup Final at Wembley with the Derby coat of arms and an inscription on the reverse. This was one of a limited number made for the players and officials. Derby won. Collecting Derby bone china and football memorabilia is an unlikely combination and this plate would probably interest the latter more. Plate without inscription £50–£100; with inscription £200–£300.

ROYAL DOULTON c.1910
Diameter 10½ins: 26.6cm Printed crown and lion.
A good quality plate with gilt work in relief, the border pale pink. Royal Doulton still produces plates of comparable quality, mainly for foreign, particularly Arab, buyers. These typically sell for £500 upwards, making old sets a cheap option. However, large numbers of single plates exist, probably made as samples.
£80–£120

ROYAL DOULTON c.1910
Diameter 10¼ins: 26cm. Printed crown and lion.
This plate is much too large for dessert, but the decoration is quite inappropriate for the main course and it was probably meant for wall display. The flower panels by C(harles). Hart, signed, who worked from 1880 to 1927, are within richly-gilt claret panels.
£200–£300

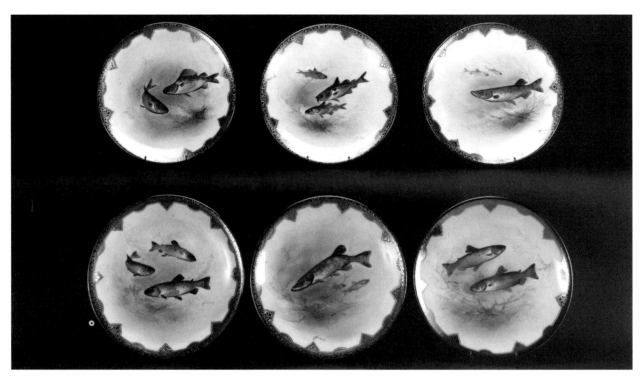

ROYAL DOULTON 1912
9ins: 23cm Printed marks.
Six from a set of twenty-four plates, each painted by F(rederick). Hancock, signed, within a gilt border.
Hancock worked at Doulton from 1879 to 1913. £2000–£3000 for twenty-four.

SAMUEL ALCOCK, Hill Pottery, Burslem c.1840
No mark.
A good quality plate and fruit stand from a frequently unrecognized factory which, despite its name, made some fine porcelain. The flowers are painted in panels on a pink ground scattered with yellow flowers and gilt scrolls. Plate £80–£120, stand £200–£300.

MINTON c.1830
Height 14½ins: 37cm No mark.
A 'spot the deliberate error piece'. It is worth studying the proportions of this tureen, cover and stand as an object lesson to be on one's guard when buying. If it looks a little uncomfortable, read no further. Originally the bowl had a foot which stood on the detachable base. The foot was damaged and the remnants ground away so that the bowl now rests fairly happily on the base. Something of a tragedy as it is a piece of the highest quality and is still decorative. The price could fluctuate wildly.
£300–£1000

MINTON c.1860
Width 13½ins: 34.4cm. Painted ermine mark.
A turquoise-ground salver painted with two fighting stags. A large decorative item and ideal for display. Both Coalport and Minton achieved great success with the turquoise glaze in imitation of Sèvres in the middle of the century. Minton's was less prone to black firing specks.
£800–£1200

159

MINTON 1851
Height 6½ins: 16.5cm Impressed name and date code.
A clumsily-moulded figure holding a shell for use as a sweetmeat or salt, uncoloured but for touches of celadon. The same figure can be found in majolica. Compare with the Worcester figure on page 64. Pair with male, £300–£500

MINTON 1861-1875
Plates 9¾ins: 25cm Impressed and printed marks and date cyphers.
A spectacular dessert service brilliantly painted, probably by Henry Mitchell, with a very popular subject – animals. Mitchell specialised in animal subjects, particularly dogs, and his works were included in the International Exhibitions between 1862 and 1875. The fact that there is a fourteen year span of date codes does not imply a made-up service, nor that it took fourteen years to paint, it simply means that Mitchell took blanks from a new and elderly stock, although this is an unusually high discrepancy.
£8000–£10000

MINTON 1870
Impressed name, retailer's mark, date code.
A fine quality tureen, cover and stand and a meat dish, but too dull for display. The crest makes it unsuitable for table use. The borders are in turquoise with matt and burnished acid-etched gilding. The 'Acid Gold' technique was patented in 1863 and bought by Minton. It was one of the techniques that gave it the edge over other manufacturers. Dish £100–£150, tureen £200–£300, plates £50.

MINTON 1872
Diameter 9¾ins: 24.8cm Printed and impressed name, date code.
A well painted plate by Henry Mitchell, signed with initials. The Pomeranian is seated within a pierced gilt border and *bleu céleste* band. Dogs and other pets are popular subject matter and to a collector of Minton *and* Pomeranians, this plate would be the ultimate prize.
£600–£800

MINTONS 1874
Printed crowned globe, impressed name, date code.
A dessert plate well-painted with fruit within an etched matt and burnished gilt border.
£180–£250

MINTONS 1878
Diameter 10⅛ins: 25.7cm Impressed name and printed Paris Exhibition mark.
A well-painted plate with a scene of French soldiers drilling on a quay within a brilliant turquoise border gilt with scrolls and oak leaves. It pays direct homage to French porcelain. The form is taken from Sèvres, as is the *bleu céleste* border, and the painting owes much to Paris porcelain of the early 19th century. There is every possibility that this was Mintons' quiet way of cocking a snook at the French as English porcelain was, at this date, far better than anything French. The mark used for this exhibition included three ostrich feathers.
£600–£900

MINTONS 1880
Diameter 9½ins: 24cm Gilt printed and impressed crown and globe, date code.
A well painted plate by L (ouis Marc). Solon, signed and dated. Instead of being in the usual white this example has a sepia-tinged girl with cream-bordered gown, chocolate scarf, pink hearts, pale blue thread and green cacti on the olive-green ground. The large number of colours could have been cloying, but is successful. In addition, Solon executed few plates, most being made by his assistants, making this a rare piece. The difficult technique of pâte-sur-pâte was made even more hazardous here by the use of polychrome. Different colours would normally need different firing temperatures and may have different co-efficients of expansion, making success a risky business.
£800–£1200

MINTON 1881
Diameter 9½ins: 24cm Impressed name, retailer's mark, date code.
A superbly painted plate by Antonin Boullemier, signed, with a girl in contemporary costume, one from a set of nine with similar subjects. The rim is gilt. A set such as this would now be split and sold as pairs or singles to collectors who would be unlikely to want the whole set. However, in this case the result would be annoying, as the scene would seem to leave a mystery hanging in the air. What horror has surprised the girl and her dog in the wood? It is unlikely that Boullemier invented these scenes, they were probably taken from illustrations to a novel of the period.
£700–£1000 single

MINTONS 1888
Impressed name, date code, printed Phillips of Oxford St., retailer's mark.
A superb quality service to which no photograph could do justice. The deep blue ground has been finely painted with gilt leaves and flowers in grey and white. Strong designs such as this, influenced by Japanese art, fall unhappily between two conflicting collecting areas. Those with a love of fine bone china (mostly women), want pretty flowers, delicately painted. For them this would be too masculine in feel. Conversely, those collecting Japonism and strong designs of the period would be less keen on the technique and material.
£80–£120

MINTONS c.1895
Diameter 9⅜ins: 24cm Printed crowned globe.
An unusual plate with white pâte-sur-pâte decoration on a black ground, the rim in salmon-pink and gilding. Louis Marc Solon, who executed this dish, signed it, as always, L. Solon, which has led to some confusion. His son, Léon, also worked for Mintons and in pâte-sur-pâte. While Solon *père* was at Sèvres, where he developed the technique on hard paste porcelain, he signed his work MILES.
£500–£700

MINTONS c.1895
Diameter 9½ins: 24cm Printed and impressed crown and globe, blurred date code.
A fine pâte-sur-pâte plate, unsigned and by one of Solon's assistants. The amusing and attractive subject is painted against a dove-grey ground. The impressed date codes on late 19th and early 20th century plates are often lightly impressed and can fill with glaze. The series with a numeral inside a swan (1895-1900) is particularly indecipherable.
£500–£800

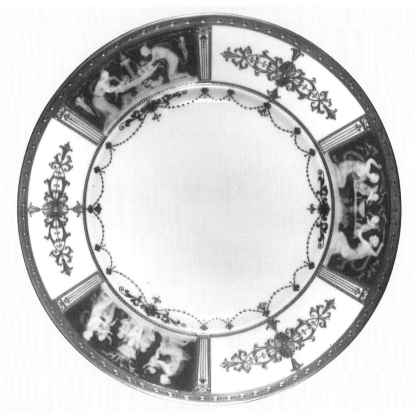

MINTONS c.1895
Diameter 10¼ins: 26cm Printed and impressed crown and globe.
A pâte-sur-pâte plate by Alboin Birks (c.1862-1940), Solon's last apprentice. The panels are of Venus and cupids against a pale blue ground and one is signed. The influence of Solon is apparent from the chosen subjects – cupids subjected to various minor tortures such as whipping, washing and roasting. Dinner plates of this type were made in quite large numbers and the scenes are well executed using a combination of moulding and hand work. The scenes are too small to excite much interest, not helped by the blank centre. However, they are known with coloured grounds and gilt scale: £500–£800

165

MINTONS 1903
Diameter 8¾ins: 22.2cm Impressed name, date cypher.
This dessert plate is painted by Leslie Johnson, signed, who is not recorded as a Minton artist. Numbers of plates with romantic ladies languishing in interiors, gardens or landscapes are met with, usually from the Berlin factory. The English painters, often amateurs, as may be the case here although the handling is quite skilful, were rarely as successful. A comparable Continental plate would be £700–£900.
£600–£800

MOORE 1892
Diameter 9ins: 23cm Printed name.
An elaborately moulded plate looking suspiciously like Royal Worcester with printed gilding and coloured flowers. The Royal Worcester influence was strong at the end of the 19th century, not only over the smaller Stoke factories but also on the Continent. Copies from Vienna, Rudolfstadt and Limoges come quite close to the originals, but the quality is less good.
£100–£150

NANTGARW 1813-1822
Diameter 9½ins: 24.1cm Impressed name.
A London-decorated Nantgarw plate with
enamelled birds in the centre. The bright
blue border is gilt with leaves. Swansea and
Nantgarw were strongly influenced by
Sèvres, trying to emulate the soft paste of
the body (which they achieved admirably)
and in the quality of the painting (which
they did less often). Pieces were expensive
at the time and remain so.
£1200–£1800

NANTGARW 1813-1822
Width 9½ins: 24cm Impressed name.
A superb dish from the justly celebrated
service belonging to the Mackintosh of
Mackintosh, chief of the Clan Chatton of
Moy Hall, Inverness-shire. The service was
painted in London with different exotic
birds within a flower-painted and gilt
border. Pieces rarely appear on the market
and when they do, fetch high prices.
£2000–£3000

NANTGARW 1813-1822
Diameter 9¾ins: 24.8cm. Impressed name.
A brilliantly-decorated plate painted in London with a vase of flowers. The border is moulded and gilt with scrolls and panels of coloured flowers on a buff ground. The quality, rarity and sheer exuberance make this a very desirable plate.
£2500–£3000

NANTGARW c. 1820
9¼ins: 23.5cm Impressed mark.
A rare Sèvres-style plate decorated in London. The birds are enclosed in a border of blue and gilt bands interspersed with rose sprigs, cornflowers and pansies. The angular birds are typical of the period and many later English-decorated Sèvres blanks are similarly painted, some by Thomas Martin Randall at Madeley.
£1500–£2000

ROCKINGHAM 1826-1830
Diameter 11½ins: 29.2cm Printed griffin in red.
A fairly standard Rockingham plate with
moulded border and broad yellow band with
trellis and leaves.
£150–£200

ROCKINGHAM 1826-1830
Diameter 13ins: 33cm Printed griffin in red.
A rare and desirable, well-painted dish with a
wide gilt rim enclosing colourful exotic birds
in a classical landscape. The value would
have been enhanced by decorative gilding.
£500–£800

169

ROCKINGHAM 1826-1830

Diameter 9½ins: 24cm Griffin in red.
A well painted spray is here enclosed by a
deep green band with gilt ears of wheat and
insects. The factory was fond of deep colours
which have a 'wet' and 'sticky' look, and rich
gilding in the early period of the factory's
production.
£180–£250

ROCKINGHAM 1830-1842

Diameter 9¼ins: 23.5cm Printed griffin in puce.
Plates with C-scroll moulding are not
uncommon and here the moulding has been
emphasised with bold and busy painting of
the border. In fact, it swamps the well-
painted landscape. A similar plate with a
spray of flowers in the centre would be
£150–£200.
£200–£400

SPODE c.1800
9ins: 23cm Painted titles and Spode.

Part of a service which includes twelve plates, each well painted with English, Irish and Scottish scenes. Such a service would lend itself to being broken up. A regular fair exhibitor would then take parts of the service to the appropriate area where local interest would enable the price to be increased by half as much again. If pairs could be formed, both in the area, the price would double.
£2500–£3000

SWANSEA early 19th century
Diameter 7¼ ins: 18.5cm No mark.

An uncommon Swansea tureen, cover and stand with a pale green border adding considerably to the price. The scarcity of large pieces from Swansea services generates much interest when they appear on the market. Apart from there being fewer tureens in a service, collectors display them in cabinets and need major items to break up the rows of plates. The translucency of Swansea at this date has been described as being 'like sodden snow'. It is clearer than any other factory at this date and imitates Sèvres very well, an ambition it came close to achieving.
£1200–£1800

SWANSEA 1814-1826
9ins: 23cm No mark.
Swansea made little use of transfer-printing, this
'Mandarin' pattern being the most elaborate. It is also very
much out of character for a factory that mainly depicted
flowers. The black design is hand-coloured with a
Chinese-style subject, popular about thirty years earlier.
Variations of the design exist, some having a coat of arms
in one of the border reserves, such as that made for
Thomas Lloyd, probably in 1819. One of these would
make £1000.
£400–£600

SWANSEA 1814-1826
Impressed name.
A fine dessert service, painted in the manner of David Evans in bright deep colours. Swansea sets are
increasingly hard to find as they are broken up for collectors. Pair of sauce tureens, covers and stands,
£2000–£3000. Large centre dish £1000–£1500. Other dishes £700–£1000, plates £600–£900.

SWANSEA c.1814-1826
Diameter 7ins: 17.8cm Red transferred name.
A fine pierced fruit stand, the bowl and base both cut with lozenges and hoops. The flowers are painted by David Evans and with good gilding. Altogether a rare and desirable piece. The huge collection of Swansea and other Welsh ceramics, formed by Sir Leslie Joseph and sold by Sotheby's in 1992, revolutionised the price structure and it looks as if these prices will hold.
£1200–£1800

WEDGWOOD c.1815
8½ ins: 21.5cm Printed name.
A rare bone china dessert plate printed and painted with botanical flowers within a gilt border. This pattern was revived at the end of the 19th century and a late plate would fetch £30–£50.

173

WEDGWOOD 1908-1912
Printed name.
A bone china dish from the dessert service specially commissioned by the 11th Duke of Bedford for his yacht. It was painted by J. P. Thornley, signed, each with a putto below the crest. The whole design, shape, vine leaf border and putto recreate the late 18th century neo-classical style, although an original would have been in creamware.
£500–£800

WEDGWOOD c.1920
Diameter 9ins: 23cm Printed vase and name.
This plate has a gilt-printed scene on a powder-blue ground. The sprayed background was adopted from Chinese powder-blue, a technique in which the cobalt was blown through gauze over the end of a bamboo tube. In the 1920s, the Kangxi (1622-1722) originals were in fashion and here Wedgwood has tried, unsuccessfully, to emulate them. Despite the magic of the Wedgwood name, they are unpopular with collectors.
£30–£40

WEDGWOOD 1920s
Diameter 10½ins: 26.8cm Printed vase and name. W559.
Although all Fairyland plates are uncommon, this pattern, *Roc Centre*, with pixies crossing a bridge is the most frequently seen. The border of gilt fairies and flowers on an apricot band is typical. The underside is usually a mottled single colour: mauve, blue or pearl, rarely with further gilding. A similar plate with brighter colour and better gilding, £800.
£500–£700

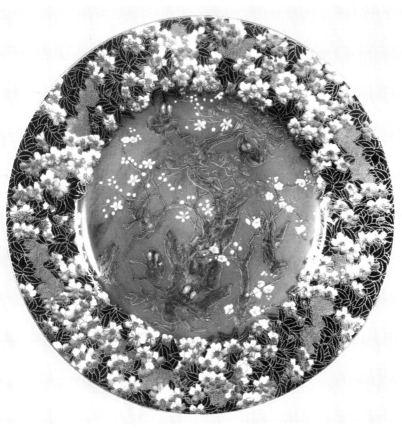

WEDGWOOD 1920s
Diameter 10⅝ins: 27cm Printed vase in gilding.
The centre of this plate with the pixies against a red ground, the rim with white and blue flowers on a black ground. Not a common pattern.
£700–£1000

**WORCESTER, BARR,
FLIGHT and BARR
1807-1813**

*9⅜ins: 24cm Impressed BFB and
crown, printed Coventry Street
address.*

A richly decorated and
colouful dessert set of ten
plates, Regency flamboyancy at
its very best. While their
impact is undoubted, eating off
them might have been less
appealing.
£1500–£2000

**WORCESTER, FLIGHT,
BARR and BARR
c.1815-1820**

*Diameter 8ins: 20.3cm Printed
name.*

A dessert plate with a 'Japan'
fence pattern in underglaze
blue and bright enamels and
gilding. Regency homages to
China and Japan have an
endearingly dotty quality
which collectors, particularly
in America, find irresistible.
They mix motifs from both
countries with panache and
the bold colouring makes them
ideal for display. In this
example an 'Alice in
Wonderland' sense of scale is
particularly appealing.
£150–£200

WORCESTER, FLIGHT, BARR and BARR c.1816
8¼ins: 21cm Impressed crowned FBB and Coventry Street address.
An interesting plate from a service made for the East India Company and bearing their arms within a pink border. British armorial plates would seem to be an area for selective collecting – they are often underpriced.
£300–£500

WORCESTER, FLIGHT, BARR and BARR c.1820
Diameter 7½ins: 19cm Printed name.
A sauce tureen, cover and stand with a rose within gilt scrolls on an apple-green ground. Not a particularly exciting piece but the gilding is of good quality as usual. The gilt pastry-mould rim is a typical Worcester feature at this date.
£400–£600

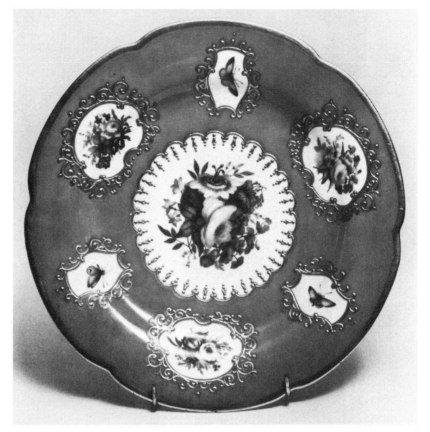

WORCESTER, FLIGHT, BARR and BARR c.1825-1830
Diameter 9ins: 23cm Printed name.
An apple-green-ground dessert plate with finely-painted flowers and insects within raised gilt scrolls. Raised gilding is very prone to wear and plates are rarely found in pristine condition, resulting in a high price when they are.
£400–£600

WORCESTER, FLIGHT, BARR and BARR c.1825
Diameter 9ins: 23cm Painted name.
Another apple-green-ground plate with a gilt pie-crust rim and border enclosing a dog-rose. Less well painted than the previous plate and the jelly-fishy outline of the panel is not appealing. The layout is more modern and a transition from the small panels round the centre found in the 18th century to the Victorian conception of a central bold spray or landscape.
£150–£250

WORCESTER, FLIGHT, BARR and BARR c.1830-1840
Diameter 10ins: 25.5cm Printed name.
A brightly-enamelled plate with the arms of Barette of India within an apple-green border. Odd survivals from armorial services such as this are not uncommon and when found are usually scratched or worn. The elaborateness of the arms affects the price considerably: a bold achievement filling the well and from a good family would fetch more than one which is smaller and less interesting; a crested plate can be bought for £50–£100.
£300–£500

WORCESTER, FLIGHT, BARR and BARR, c.1830
Diameter 7½ins: 19cm Printed name.
A version of the relief-moulded and painted plate made by Worcester in the 18th century and known as the 'Blind Earl' pattern. It was also made by Chelsea, Derby, Chamberlain's and Royal Worcester and is still in production. The story went that the design was made for the blind Earl of Coventry who enjoyed the 'Braille' roses. Unfortunately for romantics, the Earl went blind twenty-five years after the plate first appeared at Chelsea.
£200–£400

179

ROYAL WORCESTER 1868
Diameter 9½ins: 24cm Impressed and printed crowned circle, date code.
A well-painted plate with a view, named on the reverse, and one from a set of various English and Scottish views. The rims are pierced and gilt on a turquoise band.
£150–£200

ROYAL WORCESTER 1891
Diameter 9¼ins: 23.5cm Printed crowned circle, date code.
A shell dish with printed gilding and coloured flowers on an ivory ground, typical of the generality of Worcester products at the turn of the century.
£150–£250

ROYAL WORCESTER 1897
Diameter 8¾ins: 22.2cm Printed crowned circle, date code.
This somewhat impractical plate has a pierced, bronzed rim enclosing pink orchids, green leaves and masses of gilding. The shape can also be found painted by Baldwyn (£500–£700) or Stinton (£300–£400).

ROYAL WORCESTER 1898
Printed crowned circle, registration, date code.
A plate and tureen, cover and stand from a game service, each piece typically decorated with a different game bird, brightly coloured over a brown outline, the border also sepia. The handles with the amusing variation of deers' heads. While the plate would be quite acceptable to any collector, the 'animal rights' question has made the tureen a less saleable item than it might have been. Plate £100, tureen £250–£300.

ROYAL WORCESTER
1904
Diameter 10¼ins: 26cm Printed crowned circle, date code, retailer's mark.
A pastry-moulded gilt rim, borrowed from the early 19th century, here encloses a dark-green border and a large bouquet of summer flowers.
£120–£180

ROYAL WORCESTER
1907
Length 10¾ins: 27.3cm Printed crowned circle, Hadley monogram, date code.
The decoration on this dish is after William Powell and bears his 'signature'. This class of Worcester porcelain is somewhat deceptive as the artist's signature, along with the outline, was transfer-printed. Less skilled labour could then fill in the outlines in colours quickly and cheaply. The result appears to be entirely hand-painted. Peacocks are considered to be unlucky and still today there is some resistance to porcelain decorated with the birds.
£250–£350

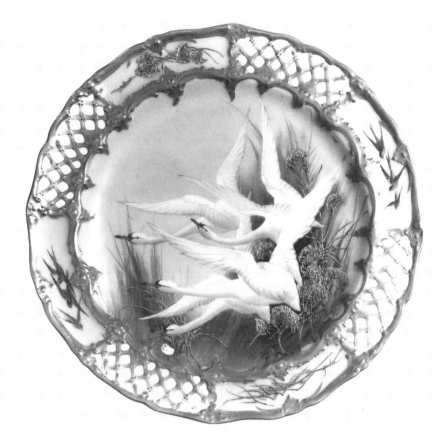

ROYAL WORCESTER
1908
Diameter 8½ins: 21.6cm Printed crowned circle, date code.
This plate has a pierced rim and is painted by C(harles). Baldwyn, signed, with his typical swans against a pale blue sky. The foreground has, more unusually, raised gilt plants. Baldwyn has a great following amongst Worcester collectors. His work is not common and is always of a high standard. Swans were his favourite bird and his handling of the white is masterly. His work is particularly popular in Australia, where Worcester is the most saleable factory.
£600–£800

ROYAL WORCESTER
1911
Width 9½ins: 24cm Printed crowned circle, date code.
A dessert dish painted by J(ames). Stinton, signed, with a misty lakeside. The deep blue border has an acid-etched gilt rim.
£250–£350

ROYAL WORCESTER
1912
Printed crowned circle, date code.
A typical tureen from a mass-produced service of the period and comparable to similar services made today. The design is a printed variation of the Indian Tree pattern with hand colouring.
£150–£250

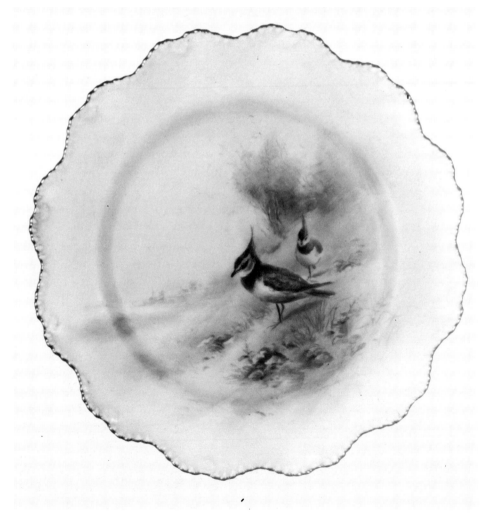

ROYAL WORCESTER
1912-1914
Printed crowned circle, date code.
A dessert plate painted rather weakly with a game bird by James Stinton, signed.
£200–£300

ROYAL WORCESTER 1918
Diameter 9½ins: 24cm Printed crowned circle, date code.
A well-painted plate by A(lbert J.). Shuck, signed, with fruit within a gilt border of pink panels on a blue ground. This was a standard pattern at Royal Worcester and amongst the most elaborate and rich they made. Their high quality makes them deservedly popular, particularly in America.
£300–£400

ROYAL WORCESTER 1926
Width 8¼ins: 20.9cm Printed crowned circle, date code.
A definite period piece of a type which is just beginning to achieve recognition. The 1920s and 1930s figures, see page 70 are already popular but the painted wares are lagging behind. This romantic scene of a girl in an Italian landscape is by (Thomas) Sedgley, signed, and is akin to many book illustrations, prints and biscuit tins of the period.
£250–£300

**ROYAL WORCESTER
1939**
*Diameter 9¼ins: 23.5cm Printed
crowned circle, date code.*
This dessert plate is painted by
R (ichard [Dick]). Sebright,
signed, with rich fruit within a
gilt-scrolled, powder-blue
ground. The border is less
elaborate than that on page
185. Worcester is still producing fruit-painted plates (at
over £100), but the quality is
not as high.
£400–£600

JOHN ROSE c.1810
Plate 8½ins: 21.6cm No mark.
Part of a dessert service described in Sotheby's catalogue quite rightly as 'sumptuous'. It was sold in 1986
when the thirty-five pieces fetched £7000. A single would now make £300–£500. What made this set
remarkable was the lack of wear, it is unlikely ever to have seen much use, probably as intended. Set
£15000–£20000.

UNATTRIBUTED c.1870
Diameter 9ins: 22.9cm No mark.
Although at first sight this dessert plate is of good quality and quite attractive, the painting of the flowers is weak. The pink ribbon, which has a transferred pink outline, runs from gilt, pierced quatrefoils and results in the whole having a somewhat anaemic look.
£80–£100

UNATTRIBUTED c.1880
Diameter 9⅛ins: 23.2cm Impressed blurred name.
A pair of plates by W. Jones, signed, on Continental blanks. A William Butley Jones worked at Royal Worcester from 1872 until 1883 as a 'decorator'. It may be that he then worked as a freelance. The lack of a firm attribution and the uncomfortable transition of scale between the two plates does not work in their favour.
£400–£600

UNATTRIBUTED c. 1882
Diameter 8¼ins: 21.3cm Painted mark.
An interesting plate painted by James Callowhill, a Worcester artist who emigrated to America with his brother in 1882. This unmarked, possibly American, plate is covered with a rich blue glaze decorated with tooled gilding and touches of pink and green enamels. The shells have been influenced by Japanese lacquer of the period. Although rare, it is less desirable than if it had been on a marked Royal Worcester body, then fetching £400–£600.
£150–£250

POT-POURRI AND PASTILLE BURNERS

As late as the middle of the last century, open sewers were running through London and the huge volume of horse traffic added to the olfactory problem. In 1858, Parliament was obliged to rise in 'The Great Stink', due to the smell from the Thames, which was practically a flood of untreated effluent. There was considerable skill needed in locating a house for the wealthy so that waste could be flushed into a nearby stream while ensuring that the smell was not brought back on the prevailing wind. When it was, high living took on a new, less appealing, meaning.

To counteract this, the upper and middle classes burned incense in pastille burners or opened the lids of their pot-pourris to let out heavier, more pleasant odours. The pellet of incense was usually placed on a depression in the base of a miniature house and the smoke wreathed out through the chimneys and windows. The Regency examples (most common) reflected all the prevailing architectural fashions, although the rustic cottage was the most popular. All are now very sought after. The idea of perfuming a room did not die out once Sir Henry Doulton had got to work with his stoneware drainpipes, and pot-pourris and rose bowls (for petals, not for displaying them) have continued to be popular.

BROWN-WESTHEAD, MOORE & Co. c.1890
Height 20½ins: 52cm Impressed name.
A good pair of pot-pourri vases from a factory better known for its useful earthenwares than fine porcelain. They exhibited frequently and received much praise for their products in the second half of the century. Here the decoration is in thick gold, silver and black against a rose ground, the neck pierced. The paste they used is very soft, prone to crazing and discoloration, although this pair of vases shows little sign of these defects. It is unlikely that a collector exists who devotes his collecting to this factory and such pieces would be bought for their decorative value.
£600–£800

DERBY c.1820
5½ins: 14cm Painted red batons and crown.
A pair of pot-pourri vases and covers with Imari coloration. The body has slightly browned, as is common at the time, compare with the Davenport example, page 203.
£400–£600

GRAINGER & Co. c.1840
Height 4ins: 10cm Painted script name.
A rare, yellow-ground, miniature pot-pourri basket and cover. The reserve is well painted with a named view of Spetchley House, near Worcester. Yellow is a rare and desirable colour and the price would be about two-thirds for a blue example.
£700–£1000

MINTON c.1835

Height 10ins: 25.4cm Painted name and crossed swords in underglaze-blue.

An attractively painted 'Globe' pot-pourri, shape 19, with a named scene of Buildwas Abbey, Salop. (Shropshire), on one side and a bouquet of flowers on the other, the whole surrounded by encrusted flowers. The practice of copying the Meissen crossed swords was endemic throughout Europe in the 18th and 19th centuries, laws only being introduced late in the 19th century to copyright trademarks. In most cases the object itself was not copied, but see page 42, top. As so often, the flowers on this example are quite nibbled; unless disfiguring, some chipping is acceptable. £600–£800

MINTON 1869

Height 13½ins: 34.2cm Impressed name and date code

A good pot-pourri, after a Sèvres original. The well-painted figure subjects are reserved on a *bleu-céleste* ground. It is easy to see why Sèvres was such an influential factory on the Victorian potters. The technical challenge of reproducing pieces as elaborate as this would have excited them considerably. Large, good quality objects are consistently strong sellers. £1500–£2000

ROCKINGHAM 1830-1842
Base diameter 3¾ins: 10cm Height 6¾ins: 17cm Marked C1 2 in gilding.
An unusual pastille burner. The bulbous perforated cover rests on a slightly raised platform on the saucer base. The moulded decoration is picked out in gilding and the flower sprays are enamelled. The same form can also be found encrusted with flowers, which make it rather more appealing.
£400–£600

ROCKINGHAM 1830-1842
Height 11ins: 27.7cm Printed griffin in puce.
A pot-pourri vase of campana form painted with a landscape on one side and flowers on the other. Unusually, the encrusted flowers have been left in the white.
£1200–£1800

SPODE c.1825
Height 3ins: 7.6cm No mark.
A miniature pot-pourri in the form of a basket and cover, the deep-blue ground with gilt scales and painted with flowers. Gilt scales on a blue ground were a feature of Spode at this date. Although unmarked, the pattern number 1166 is present, tying in with marked specimens.
£300–£500

STAFFORDSHIRE c.1830
7½ins: 19cm Unmarked.
An amusing and rare pastille burner in the form of a lighthouse encrusted with green lichen. The clue to its function is the scoops from the base and the piercings, to let air in and perfume out, respectively. Quirky objects of this kind find a ready sale.
£500–£1000

WORCESTER, FLIGHT, BARR and BARR c.1825
Height 6½ins: 16.5cm Printed name.
An extremely rare and attractive night-light cum pastille-burner in the form of a cottage which detaches from its grassy base. The windows glow realistically with a candle inside. The whole is well painted in naturalistic colours.
£800–£1200

ROYAL WORCESTER 1882
Height 14½ins: 37 cm Printed crowned circle, date code.
These Japanese-influenced vases have pierced rims arranged so that by revolving the lids the aroma of the pot-pourri can be released. As usual, the oriental influence is not a strong selling factor.
£800–£1200

ROYAL WORCESTER 1899
Height 4¾ins: 12cm Printed crowned circle, date code.
A pot-pourri with pierced cover and inner lid. The deep-toned enamelling has details in gilding. This palette is less common and more appealing than the washed-out variety.
£180–£250

ROYAL WORCESTER 1905
Height 7¼ins: 18.4cm Printed crowned circle, date code.
This vase was originally a Grainger shape, the moulds absorbed by Royal Worcester along with the
entire Grainger factory, which they bought out in 1889, closing the site in 1902. The Grainger forms are
usually less well finished and painted than the main factory's own products, nor are they as good as when
under Grainger's control. This vase has an unfinished look.
£300–£400

ROYAL WORCESTER 1909
Height 8ins: 20.3cm Printed crowned circle, date code.
A good pot-pourri with crisp moulding, coloured in shades of pink, green and orange with gilding. Others of smaller size are more frequently found, but are less desirable, as are those with the Gothic scrolling less well finished.
£400–£600

ROYAL WORCESTER 1924
Height 11½ins: 29cm Printed crowned circle and date code.
A large and decorative pot-pourri painted by J(ohn). Stinton, signed. The pierced neck is picked out in bronzes and golds. The swags on this not uncommon pattern are particularly vulnerable to damage and are often restored, as are the knops. With slight restoration £1500–£2000. The shape is still made today, fully decorated by hand with fruit and would cost the same as an old example. At this price the earlier examples seem inexpensive, as the quality of the modern pieces is nowhere near as high.
£2000–£3000

UNATTRIBUTED first quarter of the 19th century
Height 5¼ins: 13.2cm No mark.
An unusual arbour group of a boy under a lilac trellis encrusted with flowers and moss, the base with a gilt line border. The lilac ground is, as always, an important selling factor. Other colours £200–£300.
£300–£400

UNATTRIBUTED c.1825
Height 7ins: 17.8cm No mark.
An amusing pastille burner with green roof encrusted with flowers, the brown base with gilding and an arbour. The naïve construction and childlike simplicity of the flower modelling makes this a most desirable piece. All ceramic cottages, ruins and castles are now strong sellers, having had an earlier revival in the 1920s. Forgeries made then, and later, abound. Artificial ageing, particularly a fine crazing stained (usually with coffee) is common. The colouring on copies is less well handled and the casting less well defined than on the originals.
£400–£600

UNATTRIBUTED c.1830
Height 8¼ins: 21cm No mark.
An amusing lilac castle pastille burner with coloured encrustation and gilding. The leaning tower is accidental, having occurred during firing, something the tree support on the right was meant to have prevented. Here it merely adds to the charm. Other colours from £250–£400.
£400–£600

UNATTRIBUTED c.1840
Height 4ins: 10cm No mark.
A pastille burner of reasonably good quality with small flowers on a lavender ground, making this a desirable piece. As can be seen, the lid is chipped, a perfect example £400. Note that such burners were once sold as Rockingham, which they are not. The factory never used the shredded clay technique simulating moss or the wool on sheep or on dogs.
£150–£200

COALPORT (attributed) c.1835
6½ins: 16.5cm Unmarked.
A flower-encrusted pot-pourri with the piercing extending down the body – an uncommon feature. The fact that it is formed entirely of rococo scrolls and leaves is also unusual, most have a recognisable vase or ewer as a basic structure. It comes close to some of the Chelsea gold anchor wares of the 1770s in its emphasis of natural forms.
£400–£600

DAVENPORT c.1835

6¼ins: 16cm high Printed in red 'Davenport, Longport, Staffordshire'.

A pastille burner whose form has been lifted, along with the Imari-style decoration, from a contemporary Derby original. Such copying was common amongst the factories and a successful design could be used by several makers. The shape was obviously popular as numerous Derby examples exist, most lacking their lids and often suffering from the usual Derby problem of the time – discoloration. This Davenport piece is in a good state and is rarer than Derby.

£350–£550

TEA AND COFFEE SERVICES

The importance paid to the English tea ceremony in the 18th century (quite as ritualistic in its way as the Japanese equivalent) continued into the first half of the 19th. Hostesses tried to outshine each other with the magnificence and up-to-dateness of their service. The result of this one-upmanship, combined with cackhandedness, is thousands of part services. The teapot was used if there was only one visitor and was therefore the most vulnerable; teapots in good condition are scarce. A typical make-up included, besides the teapot, a milk jug, sucrier with its cover, slop bowl (often of large size) and eighteen tea cups, eighteen coffee cans (of cylindrical form) and eighteen saucers, which did service for both coffee and tea. Occasionally the teapot had a stand, and in the 18th century many had a spoon tray. Most factories painted a pattern number on the base of each piece to enable replacements to be made easily. Factory marks increased in number throughout the century, but large numbers were still being made anonymously, usually at the bottom end of the market. Differing date codes may indicate a later replacement, but if only out by a few years, probably mean no more than inefficient warehousing before sending to the retailers.

Tea plates did not come into common use until the 1870s, small plates before then were from breakfast sets. This is a reliable guide to dating, but occasionally plates were made to match an old set still in use. Invariably, close examination will reveal variations in paste, decoration or gilding. The lack of plates meant that saucers had to be both deep and large and without a locating well for the cup. A biscuit could then be lodged in the saucer with the cup slipped to one side. It was also quite acceptable to pour one's tea into the saucer to cool it. At this point there is disagreement. Was it polite to drink from the saucer, or was it poured back into the cup?

Few collectors today can house whole services and it is common practice to break them up. Apart from the major pieces, the most favoured combination is the trio: tea cup, coffee can and saucer. Tea cups must have saucers, coffee cans are still saleable without them.

BELLEEK c.1870
Printed crest.
This cup and saucer is from the first period (1863 to 1891) when the mark was the dog, tower and harp without the words 'Co. Fermanagh, Ireland'. Although the division is arbitrary, the earlier pieces are better quality, compare with page 209. It is crisply moulded under a nacreous glaze. Milk jug £80–£120; sucrier £80–£120, bowl £70–£100; cake plate £100–£200. The teapot is illustrated below.

BELLEEK c.1870
Width 8ins: 20.4cm Printed crest.
The grasses on this teapot are coloured, but untinted examples are common and about half the price. Strictly speaking, this is a kettle, which has an overhead handle, not a teapot, which has the handle at the side. They are not uncommon and large numbers must have been sold separately from the rest of the service. Despite the extraordinary thinness and apparent fragility, Belleek prided itself on its teawares withstanding boiling water. £200–£300

COALPORT c.1805
Unmarked.
A good coffee can, flamboyantly painted with summer flowers above basket weave. Despite slight wear, very desirable.
£300–£500

ANSTICE, HORTON AND ROSE, COALPORT c.1810-1815
6¾ins: 17.1cm Pattern no. 1297.
A teapot of oval cushion form boldly decorated in a pattern which distantly owes its origin to Japanese Imari. Distinguishing which factory made what with almost all tea wares of the period 1790-1835 can be a lengthy and often fruitless exercise. In this case the two Coalport factories, Anstice, Horton and Rose and John Rose, both made very similar forms which differ mainly in the shape of the knop and the bridge linking spout and body. The pattern number here confirms the attribution; John Rose's numbers reached 1000 and then became fractional. For a trio see overleaf. £300–£400

ANSTICE, HORTON AND ROSE, COALPORT c.1810-1815
A trio matching the teapot on the previous page. The tea cup is of unusual truncated, straight-sided conical form, made both by Coalport and Derby. £100–£200

COALPORT c.1860-1865
Cup height 2⅝ins: 6.7cm Painted puce ampersand mark and COALPORT.
A rare bone china cup and saucer with a so-called 'Persian' design based on Persian manuscripts and paisley shawls. Paisleys were based on Kashmir textiles, which became popular following the 1851 Great Exhibition and translated, unlike other motifs, poorly onto ceramics. The labour involved in the minute touches of enamel, and particularly the gilding, burnished and relief, must have beeen enormous. The result is surprisingly unexciting. This example with a riveted handle, £80–£120. Perfect: £150–£250.

207

BELLEEK 1872
Width 10¾ins: 27.3cm Printed crest and PODR.
This double-spouted kettle is a well-moulded, coloured and gilt first period piece. The use of sea motifs is the most obvious characteristic of Belleek, as is the nacreous (shell-like iridescent) glaze. This piece can be found with an elaborate stand in the form of a dragon on four paw feet, £1500–£2000; but watch for matched-up sections of different dates.
£700–£1000

BELLEEK c. 1875
Width 9½ins: 24.2cm Printed crest and name.
A teapot and cover of sea urchin form with a pearl-like glaze. An example with a more usual shiny glaze £150–£250; coloured £200–£300. A later period piece could be a quarter of the price.
£80–£120

BELLEEK c. 1900
second period Printed crest mark.
A second period (post-1891) moulded cup and saucer, thinly cast under a shiny glaze and with wishy-washy pink-tinged rims. It can also be found with green or gilt rims. Plate £30; teapot £100–£150; milk jug or sucrier £50; cake plate £50; cup and saucer £30.

CHAMBERLAIN'S WORCESTER c.1800
Unmarked.
A teapot, cover and stand in the 'shanked' design so popular in the late 18th/early 19th century. The restrained gilding is typical and the end result in the greyish paste is dull.
£250–£400

ROYAL CROWN DERBY
c.1900
4¾ins: 12.1cm high Printed marks.
A standard bone china, Imari pattern teapot. The quality is higher during this period than in the earlier Derby Crown Porcelain Co. period (1876-1890).
£200–£250

WILEMAN & Co., FOLEY CHINA WORKS c.1910
The Staffordshire manufacturers reflected very little of Art Nouveau and the Glasgow School under Charles Rennie Mackintosh. It was, perhaps, too *outré* for the almost moribund industry it had become. There were a few notable exceptions, of which this is one. The printed green outline has been hand-coloured and is closely based on a Glasgow design. Examples are too uncommon for there to be much of a market.
£40–£60

HAMMERSLEY & Co. c.1890
teapot 4¾ins: 12.2cm high Printed green marks and Registration number 13677.
A cup and saucer from a teaset, similarly decorated to the dressing-table set on page 107. The bold roses must have been a popular seller and, despite the registration date of 1884, it probably continued in production until the 1920s. £30–£40 cup and saucer; £80–£120 teapot.

MILES MASON c.1810
saucer 5¼ins:13.4cm Unmarked.
This is Regency abstract pattern-making at its best, with puce feathery leaves Catherine-wheeling out from chrysanthemum *mon* florets. This rare pattern would appeal to both Mason and coffee can collectors, hence the high price.
£250–£350

211

E.J.D. BODLEY 1876
Printed and impressed initials PODR.
A bone china cup and saucer from a minor factory that produced mainly useful wares. It is thinly moulded with relief sprigs of apple blossom coloured pink and with a gilt rim. The asymmetry of the design owes its origin to Japonism, then all the rage. Set of teapot, milk jug, sugar basin, four cups and saucers and tray, £300–£500.

COALPORT 1815-1820
Pattern no. 57.
Apart from the flamboyant 'Japan' patterns, the Regency produced highly attractive geometric designs, often in unlikely colour schemes, this example in iron-red, green and gilding. Green enamel was thin and needed to be applied thickly to achieve opacity. Here, the factory has applied sufficient only to provide a mottled appearance, far more attractive than a solid block would have been. Teapot £300–£500; trio £100–£200.

COALPORT 1825-1830
Tray 16¼ ins: 41.3cm Unmarked.
A solitaire (a teaset made for one – a tête-à-tête is for two, a déjeuner, breakfast set or cabaret for two or more), painted with panels of pink roses within gilt-scrolled borders and with green sprigs. Despite the crack to the handle, it is readily saleable. £1200–£1800

COPELAND 1833-1847
Printed wreath and crown, titled in red.
The panels of English and Scottish views on this cup and saucer are reasonably well painted and are named on the bottom of each piece, adding to the interest and to the price. The scenes are enclosed by gilt moulded scrolls on a pale yellow ground. Set of twelve each coffee cups, tea cups and saucers, milk jug, two cake plates, basin £1000–£1500. A teapot would fetch £300–£500.

SPODE c.1810
4¾ins: 12cm Unmarked.
A bat-printed bone china cup and saucer with a romantic ruined
castle within a gilt apricot border. Spode produced several dozen
similar landscapes. This example shows little wear compared to
most.
£100–£120

SPODE c.1820
Stand diameter 11¾ins: 29.8cm Red script name.
A rare set of tulip cups and their stand which would have been used for ices or for custards. They are outrageously decorative and always sell well. In some cases the stand is earthenware, not porcelain, but the price is unaffected. £10000–£12000

SPODE early 19th century
Unmarked.
A cup and saucer of 'Bute' shape, bat-printed in purplish-brown. This is a rare colour, a black example would be about half the price. £100–£150

DAVENPORT c.1850
Printed name and PODR.
A superbly rich cup and saucer in orange and gilding, demonstrating the high quality that this formerly neglected factory could achieve. £100–£200

DAVENPORT c.1880
Printed and impressed names, retailer's mark.
A tea and coffee service which might, at first sight, be attributed to Royal Crown Derby, which it closely copies, see page 218. The two most popular Derby Imari patterns, 1128 and 2451, were imitated by numerous factories, both in porcelain and earthenware. This Davenport example is rarer than the original but would cost much the same. Cup and saucer £50 each.

BLOOR DERBY 1825-1840
Printed circle mark.
Part of a breakfast service in an Imari palette of iron red, underglaze blue and gilding which included, amongst the usual items, six egg cups. These now have quite a following in their own right and many factories made them. Egg cup £60; cup and saucer £70; jug £60; plate £100.

**ROYAL CROWN DERBY
1899**
Printed crowned monogram, date code.
A superb quality cup, saucer and plate of 'Brighton' shape and made to order with a red, green and gilt monogram within a gilt 'rose Pompadour' border. A service of this type would probably not have had a teapot, milk jug or sucrier, these would have been silver.
Cup and saucer £80–£100; plate £200.

**ROYAL CROWN DERBY
1913**
Printed crowned monogram, date code.
Part of a cabaret service comprising the pieces shown and four cups, saucers and plates, milk jug and tray, each with the Imari 2451 pattern. The teapot is of late 18th century form.
Service £600–£800

ROYAL CROWN DERBY
1922
Printed crowned monogram and date code.
The famous Imari pattern 1128, not to be confused with the not dissimilar 2451 pattern. This is still in production and is expensive, a cup and saucer will cost £60–£80 and a lozenge-shaped plate £80–£120 compared with this example, £50 and £150. The date is immaterial and prices alter little as long is it is post-1890, when the quality improved.

MINTON 1830-1835
Painted pattern no. 724H.
Part of a tea service delicately painted with flowers within yellow gilt borders. A distinctly feminine set of good quality, hence the high price. Teapot £300–£400; trios £50–£100; plates £100–£150; sucrier and jug £150–£250; bowl £40–£60.

NEW HALL c.1810
Pattern no. 288.
A hard paste teapot and stand of neo-Classical low oval shape, the gilt leaves with iron-red berries. The hold New Hall has over its devotees is strong, even the most boring pattern will make double that of a comparable pot from another factory. £300–£500

NEW HALL c.1810-1820
11⅜ins: 29cm Pattern no. 536.
A hybrid hard-paste teapot simply decorated with underglaze-blue bands gilt with leafy trails. Somewhat dull, even for a New Hall addict. £250–£400

NEW HALL c.1815
9⅞ins: 25cm Pattern no. 984.
A teapot, bat-printed with the
'Country Scenes' pattern,
hand-coloured over black. This
example was restored, perfect
£500–£800

NEW HALL c.1815-1825
Teapot 9¾ins: 25cm Pattern nos. 1163 and 1161 (erroneously).
A service painted in underglaze-blue, pale blue and orange with an orientalised landscape. Trios
£100–£120; teapot £400–£600; plate £100–£200; bowl £80–£120; milk jug, sucrier £250–£350.

ROCKINGHAM 1826-1830
No mark.
A cup and saucer with moulded overlapping primrose leaves crudely coloured in yellow shading to green with gilt veins. Similar pieces can be found with the red or puce mark, but even when unmarked can be positively attributed as no other factory produced similar pieces. In the 18th century both Longton Hall and Chelsea used moulded, naturalistically coloured overlapping leaves. They are only marginally more successful. £120–£150

ROCKINGHAM 1826-1830
Griffin mark in red and 599.
An Empire style trio, the form similar to that of many factories, but as so often, differing enough for attributions to be made. Here the saucer has a deep foot rim and the handle is unique to Rockingham. The fashion for painting decoration on the interiors only, leaving the outside blank is not popular with collectors. £150–£200

ROCKINGHAM 1826-1830
Griffin in red and 684.
A stylish Empire design with gilt bands that seems more art deco in inspiration than a century later. The shape is rare. The handles are formed as a horse's hoof, the upper part representing the tail, a form made by no other factory.
£250–£300

ROCKINGHAM 1826-1842
Griffin mark in puce and 612.
Although this form of cup is typical of the teawares produced by Rockingham in the early period 1826-30, it was also made after this date. It is almost identical to a Ridgway example. Here the decoration is of gilt scrolls and foliage on a deep-blue ground with the larger leaves in apricot.
£60–£80

ROCKINGHAM 1830-1835
Printed griffin in puce, red pattern no. 1224.
A late service, each piece painted in grey outlined in gilding and with strawberries. Note the typical Rockingham crown knops. £600–£800

SPODE c.1805
Saucer 5¼ins: 13.6cm
Unmarked.
A rare cup and saucer with a black bat print of Admiral Lord Nelson between trophies, the saucer with a plan of the Battle of Trafalgar and made shortly afterwards to commemorate Nelson's victory.
£500–£600

SPODE c.1810
Painted name.
An extremely rare set of bone china tulip ice cups on an earthenware tray, all brilliantly enamelled on coloured or gilt bases. Ceramic flowers, fruit and vegetables are very desirable whether in Delftware, pottery or porcelain and whether oriental or European. Single cup £600–£800.
£10000–£12000

SPODE c.1820
Teapot 10½ins: 27cm Printed SPODE and pattern no. 2416.
Part of a twelve setting tea service in Imari style with 'Chinese' landscapes in red, underglaze-blue, green and gilding. The cups suffer the problem common to many of the period of bearing scant decoration on the outside, making them difficult to display. Trio £100–£150; teapot £300–£500; jug and sucrier £200–£300; bowl £50–£100.

SPODE c.1808-1812
Unmarked.
A teapot, cover and stand bat-printed on the 'New Oval' form with rural scenes. The dog is a fairly common print and is after an engraving by Samuel Howitt. The landscapes are from an untraced source, possibly a book of sketches made by a factory artist or they may be only romantic concepts of the engraver. The change of sale from large dog to landscape might today be thought uncomfortable, but such niceties were overlooked at the time. The reverse of the teapot has a print of cows which is unrecorded on wares.
£250–£400

UNATTRIBUTED c.1805
5⅜ins: 13.8cm Unmarked.
A saucer, bat-printed in black with a child lifting the veil of a swooning maid on a daybed. All terribly theatrical and Regency. The two encircling lines are in silver (platinum). £100–£200

ROYAL WORCESTER 1923
Printed crowned circle marks, impressed marks, date codes.
A boxed coffee set by H(arry). Stinton, signed, with Highland cattle. These boxed sets are ready sellers but the presence of a damaged piece, as here – one cup is cracked – makes the satisfactory sale much more problematical. It would be unlikely to make its way to the United States of America or to Australia where there is a ready market, but would probably be bought as a 'breaker', each cup and saucer being sold singly or as pairs. The silver spoons would go to a spoon collector.
£1200–£1600

SWANSEA c.1815-1817
Impressed name.
A tea service painted by William Pollard. A complete service would now be rare and any set would be likely to be broken and the pieces sold separately. Teapot £800–£1200; milk jug £300–£500; bowl £300–£400; sucrier £400–£600; trios £200–£300.

SWANSEA c.1820
Impressed name.
A superb Cabaret set, each piece painted in London in Empire style with various growing flowers and with gilt borders. Swansea came closer to the French Empire style than did any other factory in this country.
£2500–£3000

WEDGWOOD c.1815
Red stencilled name.
Josiah Wedgwood was no devotee of bone china and it was in production only from 1812-22 under
Josiah II. It was re-introduced in 1878. This cup and saucer is quite rare, the green cell diaper has
printed outline figures, hand coloured over the glaze. The ground can be found in other colours.
£150–£200

WEDGWOOD c.1890
*Width 5ins: 12.8cm. Printed
name.*
A rare bone china teapot in
neo-classical taste. The
medallion is bronzed and gilt
and the whole of fine quality
making it very desirable. It is
uncommon to find the neo-
Classical revival so purely or
satisfactorily executed in bone
china.
£500–£800

UNATTRIBUTED c.1830
4⅜ins: 11.2cm.
The making of tulip-form ice cups was all the rage in the 1820s and 1830s, some appearing on a leaf-edged tray. Many are Spode but other factories also produced them. They are highly prized by decorators and have a ready sale. This is one of a pair with slight restoration. £1000

UNATTRIBUTED c.1835-1840
Teapot 8ins: 20.2cm Pattern no. 73.
A rococo revival tea service of undistinguished quality. The gilding has been carefully painted but the overall effect is too dull for today's taste. Additionally, there is damage to the teapot and sucrier and the jug handle has been riveted. It is ripe for 'splitting' and selling off trios to cup and saucer collectors. Trio £30–£40; teapot £20–£40; sucrier £20–£30; jug £8–£10. Set in good state with eight each cups, coffee cups and saucers £400–£600.

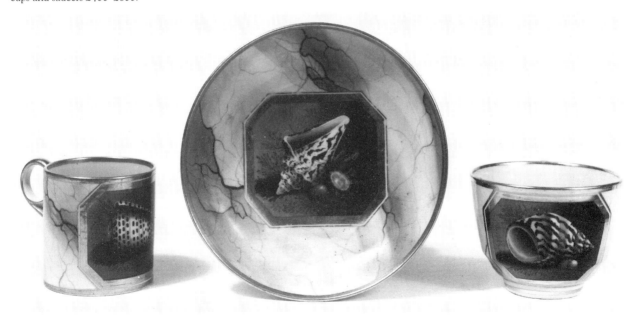

WORCESTER, BARR, FLIGHT AND BARR c.1810
Printed name.
A Barr, Flight and Barr trio, each piece finely painted with shells on a simulated grey marble ground. There were several shell painters working at Worcester, including John Barker and Samuel Smith and Thomas Baxter in London. Shell subjects have been one of the fastest risers in value in the last ten years. £1000–£1500

ROYAL WORCESTER 1881
Printed crowned circle, date code.
A reasonably painted service with coloured flowers. The jagged outline of the floral sprays is characteristic of the 1870s to 1890s as is the inclusion of ferns – cult plant of the period. Heather, inspired by Victoria and Albert's love affair with Balmoral, is also common. Undated flower painted pieces can confidently be dated from these signals. £150–£200 for these three pieces.

ROYAL WORCESTER 1890
Height 9¾ins: 24.8cm Printed crowned circle with date code.
Royal Worcester coffee pots are considerably rarer than teapots, but this example is not of the best. The colours are thin and the gilding weak on the ivory-coloured ground.
£200–£300

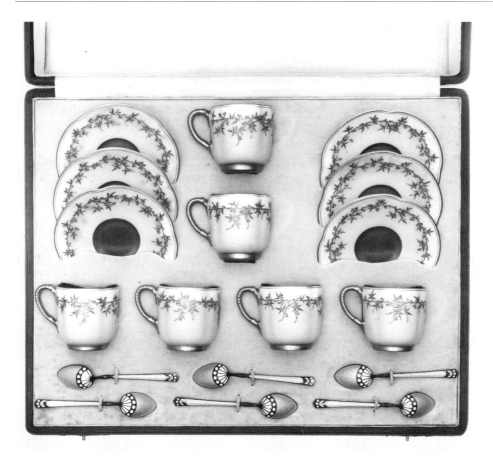

ROYAL WORCESTER
1912-1913
Printed crowned circle, date code.
This boxed set has a yellow band to each piece with raised gilt leaves and the interior, as usual, burnished gilding. The (imported) enamelled silver spoons are in art deco style, a great help to an otherwise uninspiring set. As is common, the date codes vary in the set as they were made up from stock held in quantities on a shelf. A set such as this would probably be broken by the trade, making a quicker and better profit than trying to sell the whole. A cup and saucer might be found in an antiques market for £30-£50 and a spoon £10-£15. (Set at auction) £300–£400

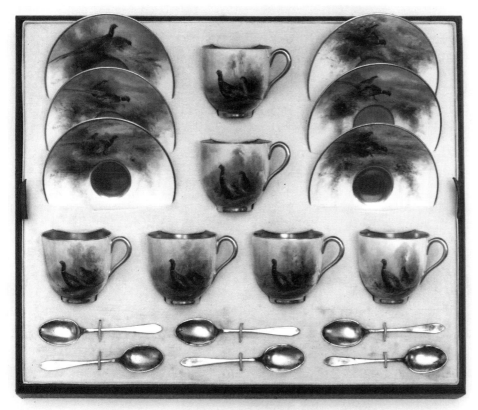

ROYAL WORCESTER
1928
Printed crowned circle, date code.
A boxed coffee set painted by James Stinton, signed, with pheasants, the interiors gilt. Such sets are now highly collectable and might either be split or sold intact, the state of the box probably being the dictating factor. In the first edition of this guide, the whole set was priced at £300–£350. £1000–£1500

SPODE c.1815
Painted red SPODE and pattern no. 2234.
A fine bone china tea service but with a too wishy-washy overall appearance. To be a strong seller the flowers would need to be more colourful and the strength of the border darker. It comprised forty-two pieces and would certainly end up divided into trios, teapot etc. and sold separately. £1500–£2000

CHAMBERLAIN'S WORCESTER c.1820
Painted marks including pattern no. 263.
A strongly decorated service with a 'Japan' pattern known as the *pseudo tobacco leaf*, but actually based on a Chinese original of the 18th century. Both this and the 'real' tobacco leaf originals are very sought after in America and, no doubt, this service would have transatlantic appeal also. The set comprised forty-four pieces of which a few were damaged. In this case the set would be more likely to remain together than to be sold individually.
£3000–£4000

ROYAL WORCESTER 1929
Printed crowned circle, date code.
An uncommon set painted by Jack Stanley with hunting scenes, much rarer than the Stintons' work or fruit subjects. Unlike the former which repeat the scenes on each piece, here every scene is different. This set would certainly be broken, largely because the mass of colour, including the huntsmens' red coats, has a cheapening effect *en masse*. £2000–£3000

ROYAL WORCESTER Various dates
Printed crowned circle, date codes.
A comparison of single cups and saucers, ignoring the spoons. a: Fruit by Edward Townsend, signed, 1934 £150–£250 . b: Powder-blue ground, gilt border 1926 £30–£50. c: Pheasants by James Stinton, signed, 1927 £180–£250. d: Transfer-printed roses, gilt-edged, green-scrolled border, pierced silver mounts, 1905 £30–£50.

VASES

The ancient Greeks made vases which were for decorative purposes only and the tradition has continued. In fact, it is rarer for a vase to have a practical use, than not. From the 18th century onwards, the vase was regarded as the object on which to lavish the best painting, gilding and modelling. The Victorian porcelain factories, in their constant search to better each other, frequently overreached themselves and produced monsters.

Today, prices are governed largely by how decorative a vase (or, preferably, a pair which is worth at least three times a single) is and, to a lesser extent, by the factory. Signed paintings, as always, help the value and most painters have been identified and their working dates recorded in factory monographs. An unsigned painting with an added signature has not yet come to notice. No doubt it will in time.

Damage, where it is not obvious, will affect the price less than on many other classes of objects. Covers are frequently broken and in some cases the form may not suggest immediately that one was originally called for. A flange inside the mouth is one obvious clue, so is an unglazed or ungilt rim where one might be expected. Many vases were potted in sections and luted together with slip. At certain times at certain factories, this was a weak point and junctions should always be carefully examined. Original metal rods are uncommon on English vases, except for large Exhibition pieces.

COALPORT c.1825
10¼ins: 26cm Unmarked.
A good vase with fine flower painting and gilding on a revived Rococo form. The degree of movement achieved by the modeller is as good as on 18th century Sèvres porcelain and presages Art Nouveau designs of seventy years later. The design appears also 15ins (38.1cm) high and was originally part of a garniture with a covered central vase. The handles are very rarely found intact and some restoration will reduce the price to £600–£800. Pair £800–£1200.

DERBY c.1880-1883

15ins: 38cm Printed crown mark.

A pair of Sèvres-style vases painted by G. Landgraff, signed, with dancing children. The quality of the work is high but the market for Sèvres-style vases was stronger in the 1970s and early '80s than it is now. Additionally, Derby is not well-known for this type of work. The covers have been restored and there is some wear to the gilding. £2000-£2500

BROWNFIELD and SON c.1875
Height 9¼ins: 23.5cm Printed globes mark.
A highly successful tinted Parian vase of a standard which the smaller Stoke factories rarely achieved. Brownfield produced mid-quality earthenwares, particularly services, stoneware and Parian. This piece is exceptionally well moulded and coloured, as well as being a cleverly conceived design, the apricot body with putty-coloured leaves and white flowers. £250–£350

BELLEEK Third quarter of the 19th century
Height 16ins: 40.6cm Black printed crest.
A rare and desirable piece of First Period Belleek, both for its large size and good coloration; it is also well moulded. An uncoloured example £800–£1200 and a late piece with 'County Fermanagh, Ireland' added to the crest £600–£900.

BROWN-WESTHEAD, MOORE & Co. c.1870
Height 23ins: 58.5cm No mark.
A fine vase with well-painted classical scenes on an apple-green
ground with flowers at the base and gilt handles. A major piece
from a factory which produced little of this quality and rivalling
Minton. Pair £1800–£2500

BROWN-WESTHEAD, MOORE & Co. c.1870
Height 15¾ins: 40cm No mark.
A high quality tinted Parian vase from a factory which produced
little in the way of major decorative pieces. The figure is left white
and is sitting on gilt and apricot sheaths forming vases. The smaller
factories would commission new designs from freelance artists such
as A. E. Carrier-Belleuse and Hugues Protât to represent their work
at the Exhibitions or for factory or retailers' display purposes.
£600–£900

CARLTONWARE c.1925
14¾ins: 37.5cm Printed marks.
Arguably one of the best pieces of Carltonware produced, this large jar inspired by the opening of Tutankhamun's tomb is transfer-printed in enamels and gilding on a powder-blue ground. Unlike Wedgwood's Fairyland Lustre, Carltonware, which lacks the famous name, has lagged behind but is gathering a strong following (as it should).
£1000–£1500

COALPORT First quarter of the 19th century
Height 4¾ins: 12cm No mark.
An attractive flower-painted vase in bright enamels reserved on a pink ground with gilt borders. It is worth comparing this vase with the Rockingham example page 269 which, although a little larger, is as well painted, but without the coloured ground.
£300–£500

COALPORT c.1840
Height 12ins: 30.5cm Painted name.
A sad example of the dying of a good vase. One handle has completely vanished, the other almost and most of the flowers have been plucked. However, the painting is good and the main body of the vase is undamaged. Restoration is out of the question as the cost would be prohibitive but with the handles ground off and filled with flowers, the damage would pass unnoticed.
£300–£500

COALPORT 1861
Height 25¼ins: 64cm Gilt ampersand mark
It is rare to be able to attribute firmly objects that were displayed in one of the International Exhibitions in the 19th century. This example was probably painted by Robert Frederick Abraham and was on show at the 1862 London Exhibition. It was illustrated in J. B. Waring's *Masterpieces of the 1862 Exhibition*. The necessity of making ceramic objects that would stand out from the crowd of other wonders meant that they had to be impressive. In most cases this was achieved at the expense of any human feeling – they can be admired, but rarely loved. They are usually bought by museums. This example was badly cracked.
£2500–£3000

COALPORT c.1861
Height 15½ins: 39.4cm CBD (Coalbrookdale) monogram.
A superb pair of rose-pompadour ground vases with brilliantly painted scenes after François Boucher. The rope handles and other details are picked out in gilding. The factory had a reputation at the time for the success of its pink ground. As is not uncommon with vases of this period, the junction of the body and foot is a weak point and the two may part. As long as there is no chipping, cracking or loss, this barely affects the price.
£2000–£3000

COALPORT c.1861
Height 30¼ins: 76.8cm Gilt ampersand.
A large and very high quality vase and cover, probably made for the 1862 Exhibition. The putti in clouds may be by James Rouse who later became a star decorator at Derby. The *bleu-céleste* ground is gilt with scrollwork.
£3000–£4000

COALPORT 1897
Height 21 ¼ins: 54cm Printed name, retailer's name, limitation number.

A large and well executed vase made to commemorate the 1897 Diamond Jubilee of Queen Victoria. The small medallions on one side are scenes typical of the time of the Coronation, and on the other the same updated, i.e. reaping by hand and then mechanically. Fifty examples were made for Ostler's of Oxford Street. One of the few exceptions to the rule that coronation or commemorative wares are of little value. In the 1975 edition of this book it was priced at £800-£1000. It would be unlikely to fetch more today. Modern, so-called Limited Editions, have all but killed the market. £1000–£1500

COALPORT c.1900
Height 7ins: 17.8cm Printed name.

A three-handled vase with good gilding on the dark blue ground enclosing small landscapes. Coalport of this date is very thinly potted and is frequently found cracked. Despite the awkwardness of some of the forms (particularly here on the foot) and the small size of the landscapes they are readily saleable.
£300–£500

COALPORT 1898
Height 7ins: 17.8cm Printed name, PODR.

A small pair of vases painted with scenes within lemon-yellow panels. The form could be faulted for its design – the bodies are too dumpy, the feet too small, the handles incongruous, but the market takes no cognisance of such judgments – they are miniatures and Coalport and that is enough.
£700–£1000

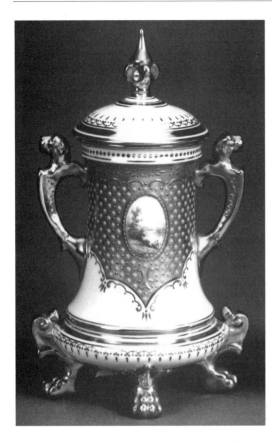

COALPORT c.1900

6¾ins: 17cm Printed marks.

One of a pair of 'jewelled' vases with small landscape panels, the ground in cream. The jewelling is formed on turquoise dots of enamel which on many pieces graduated according to the form of the vessel far more than they do here. It was a time-consuming and skilled job and such pieces are strong sellers. £1200–£1800

COALPORT c.1910

Height 10¼ins: 26.1cm Printed name, retailer's mark.

A good pair of vases and covers well painted by F(rederick). H.Chivers, signed on a royal blue ground. Fine quality Coalport has maintained a steady rise in price and is in line with prices for Royal Worcester and Royal Crown Derby (to which Chivers went after the First World War). £2000–£3000

COPELAND c.1860
Height 11ins: 28.5cm No mark.
A crisp and clean pair of Parian vases, double-walled, pierced and moulded with female masks of the sun and moon within green enamelling and gilding. Parian was known at Copeland as Statuary Porcelain, but the Minton term has superceded others. When successful, as here, Parian wares are amongst the best ceramics of the period, but do not attract the attention they deserve and are underpriced.
£800–£1200

COPELAND 1862
Height 17¼ins: 44cm Printed name.
A fine vase painted by Charles Ferdinand Hürten and exhibited at the 1862 London Exhibition. The neck and foot are painted with blue leaves and gilding on a pink ground, all of a high standard. The knop is a replacement in ormolu. Hürten was probably the best flower painter of the period, his work appearing at all the major Exhibitions. A large vase, possibly his masterpiece, is in the Victoria & Albert Museum.
£2000–£3000

COPELAND c.1870
19¾ins: 50cm Unmarked.
A superb pair of vases boldly and luxuriantly painted by C. F. Hürten, signed. They are of Exhibition standard, as is most of Hürten's work. These have hair cracks, a problem encountered on many large pieces of Copeland bone china at this date. It would seem to be an inherent instability of the paste rather than carelessness. £5000–£6000

COPELAND 1874
Height 9¾ins: 25cm Impressed name and date code.
One of a pair of amusing and well executed bone china reed warbler and bulrush vases, the nest turquoise and the rest with gilding. Cheap.
Pair £600–£800

COPELAND 1891-1902
Height 10¼ins: 26cm Printed name.
The shoulders of these vases are apple-green and gilding and the bodies are well painted with clear and naturalistic flowers by F.(W.) Adams, signed. Adams' painting is as good as that of sixty years earlier and vases of this quality at this date are not common.
£1500–£2000

COPELAND c.1900
Height 16¼ins: 41.5cm Printed name.
A richly-decorated pair of vases with 18th century figure subjects by S(amuel). Alcock, signed. The rest of the body is deep blue and gilt scrolled. Alcock was one of the better late 19th century painters and the large size of these vases makes them highly desirable. 18th century style figures, while never having quite faded from fashion during the second half of the 19th century, almost completely replaced the neo-Classical and Japonaise styles at the end, although some dogs' dinners attempt to pander to every taste.
£2500–£3000

COPELAND and GARRETT 1833-1847
Height 5ins: 12.6cm Printed wreath.
One of a pair of dainty and feminine Rococo-revival boudoir spill vases with attractive painting and gilding. Less fussy than the flower-encrusted type and very popular. Pair £500–£800.

DAVENPORT 1820-1830
Height 10½ins: 27cm Davenport Longport.
A porcelain vase in Paris Empire style decorated with raised and tooled gilt agricultural trophies on a matt blue ground. The handles are in the form of female heads and can be found with the wings touching the head, as here, or separate. The same form is found with panels of flowers, £700–£1000. Davenport came closer to reproducing the Paris style than any other Staffordshire factory. The matt blue ground, popular at the time, is amongst the few ceramic colours that are fugitive, particularly when pale, and may turn yellow or brown and eventually fade to nothing. The advantage of Davenport over the Paris originals is that the gilding fires well on English porcelain whereas it is frequently missing on hard paste. The vase, as with the Paris originals, and other Davenport of this date, was potted in two parts jointed by a rod and nut.
£800–£1200

ROYAL CROWN DERBY 1889
Height 5¾ins: 14.6cm Printed crowned monogram and date code.

Derby would here seem to be imitating Continental glass in both the washed-out yellow ground and the poorly-handled gilt flowers. The influence is Japanese but, as so often in Staffordshire at this date, it has been misunderstood. Even the Royal Crown Derby name would not help the price here. For some reason many factories produced flat, brassy gilding relieved by raised line work in the 1880s.
£250–£300

DERBY CROWN PORCELAIN COMPANY 1885
Height 18½ins: 47cm Printed crowned monogram and date code.
A superb quality vase, designed by H. Warrington Hogg, but lacking its cover. The cream ground has been decorated in pale gilding and with red and green flowers. The borders are matt and burnished gold. As with much Derby bone china at this date, it is very thinly potted. Pair with covers.
£2500–£3000

ROYAL CROWN DERBY 1891
Height 8¼ins: 20.7cm Printed crowned monogram and date code.
A pair of eccentrically-designed vases with gilt handles and decoration on a pink ground. The painting is unfortunately not of the best, with a resulting lowish price.
£300–£400

ROYAL CROWN DERBY 1892
Height 12½ins: 31.9cm Printed crowned monogram and date code.
A bottle vase decorated in a bright Imari palette with profuse gilding. Here the raised gilt outline helps the designs, in contrast to the pair on page 251. Nevertheless, the design is over busy, although that drawback is not reflected in the price – the style sells well.
£600–£800

ROYAL CROWN DERBY 1904
Height 16¾ins: 42.6cm Printed crowned monogram, date code.
An exceptionally large urn painted by W(illiam). E. Mosley, signed, with flowers on a deep blue ground gilt with scrolls. The form is closely based on a much smaller Bloor period original. The impressive size and quality of this piece would make it a strong seller. Pair £2500–£3000

ROYAL CROWN DERBY 1911
Height 5¾ins: 14.7cm Printed crowned monogram, date code.
A small vase with the 1128 Imari pattern. In a less popular design £150–£250. Pair, as illustrated £400–£600

ROYAL CROWN DERBY 1920
15⅜ins: 39cm Printed mark and date code, incised shape no. 1492.
A large vase painted by A(lbert). Gregory, signed, with a colourful panel of flowers reserved on a royal-blue ground. From the photograph, the piece could be judged to be the more usual 5ins or so. Curiously, the smaller size would be little different in price. £1500–£2000

DOULTON late 19th century
Height 11¾ins: 30cm Printed rosette.
The roses on this pair of Doulton bone china vases are against a deep blue ground with gilt leaves. Much turn-of-the-century, blue-decorated Doulton is part printed and part hand-painted and the printing is often difficult to determine. On some pieces a spray-gun has been used.
£500–£700

GRAINGER, LEE & Co. c.1830
Height, largest 11ins: 28cm Painted name.
A rare and attractive garniture of vases with panels of flowers on a deep blue ground above springing leaves. These have a pineapple feel about them and are akin to the bases of pillars on the Brighton Pavilion. Their large size and flamboyance would make them ideal decorator's material.
£1000–£1500

GRAINGER and Co. 1850-1870
Height 5½ins: 14cm Printed name.
A well fabricated pair of vases that should have covers. The bodies are pierced with good gilding and panels of flowers. With covers £700–£900
£500–£700

GRAINGER and Co. 1870-1889
Height 7⅛ins: 18cm Printed shield.
A vase and cover well-pierced by Alfred Barry and with simple gilt line details. Having lagged in price far behind George Owen's work, Grainger's piercing is slowly catching up, although there is still a huge and justifiable gap. The more elaborate the piercing the more expensive the piece will be. The matt surfaces of these wares are easily imitated by the restorer and great care should be taken when examining them.
£300–£500

GRAINGER and Co. 1870-1889
Height 10ins: 25.4cm Printed shield.
A pair of vases with a creamy matt ground relieved by a band of gilt-edged leaves and pink flowers. They lack the original covers and are a little too restrained for today's taste. With covers £700–£1000
£500–£600

GRAINGER and Co. c.1875
Height 9½ins: 24cm Printed shield.
A poor attempt at Japonism by Grainger & Co., who rarely made a success of it. The coloured sprigs and butterfly have printed outlines against the duck-egg blue ground. The sparse decoration is barely relieved by the gilt mask and snake handles. £180–£250

GRAINGER and Co. c.1880
Height 9½ins: 24cm Moulded KL monogram.
A well-decorated pâte-sur-pâte moon flask, probably by Kate Locke, one of the large family of Lockes, whose initials appear on the base. Contemporary photographs show this shape as Grainger's where the father, Edward worked for a time before he set up the short-lived Locke's Worcester factory (1895-1902) producing Royal Worcester style wares. Locke's was taken to court by Royal Worcester and they, and anyone else, were banned from using the Worcester name. £400–£600

GRAINGER and Co. 1890
Height 7¾ins: 19.8cm Printed shield and PODR.
An amusingly conceived pair of vases with piercing and gilt necks.
The inspiration here is from contemporary Indian brass ware.
£600–£800

GRAINGER and Co. 1891
Height 7½ins: 19cm Printed shield and date code.
The deep blue body of this vase is decorated with gilt and grey-blue
hops. The neck is poorly moulded and with piercing. Pair
£500–£700

GRAINGER and Co. 1891-1900
Height 12ins: 30.5cm Printed shield.
An extraordinarily eclectic pair of vases. The form is based on a
Chinese Shang dynasty bronze *ku*, although it is more likely to have
arrived via a Chinese transitional porcelain vase of the same form.
The central band is either Mughal or from 17th century German
silver and the pierced scrollwork Moorish. Considering the mess it
could have been, the result is not altogether unhappy. Examples
can be found with additional gilding, raising the price by 20%.
£600–£800

GRAINGER and Co. 1900
Height 9¼ins: 23.5cm Printed shield and date code.
A Grainger's vase of unusual form and with a Stinton-influenced Highland landscape against a peachy-yellow ground.
£300–£500

J. HADLEY & Sons 1900
Height 11ins: 28cm Printed name, date.
A tyg with coloured slip 'mounts' and painted orchids. Like most of Hadley's products, of good quality and unusual coloration. James Hadley (1837-1903) set up his own factory in Worcester in 1896, which was absorbed by the main factory in 1905.
£300–£500

GEORGE JONES 1874-1891
Height 6ins:15.3cm Impressed initials.
A pâte-sur-pâte vase decorated by F(rederick). Schenk, signed, in white against a deep green body, the ring handles gilt. Although George Jones is recognised for its majolica, the porcelain receives less attention than it deserves. While the pâte-sur-pâte is not up to the standard of Minton and some of it appears to be at least part mechanical, they made some fine pieces. Unfortunately, the forms tend to be dumpy and less elegant than Minton's.
£400–£600

Minton c.1835
Heights 9¾ins and 10½ins: 24.7cm and 26.8cm No mark.
A garniture of well- and brightly painted vases on a cobalt
blue ground and with peach and gilt handles. This set
would be an interior designer's delight, although a paler
background would be even more saleable. The dragon
handles have been taken from Chinese Canton-decorated
vases of about the same date.
£1800–£2500

MINTON c.1840
Height 28ins: 71cm No mark.
A flower-encrusted tour-de-force. It appears in the Minton
shape book as the 'Very Large Dresden Vase', shape number
230. Although unmarked it can, therefore, be attributed
firmly to the factory. The costs were also noted: £3.12.0 for
the figure painting and 5/- (25p) for the floral bouquet on
the cover. The painting is of a very high standard, as is the
modelling of the flowers. A vase such as this is unlikely to
be found in perfect condition and a little damage or
restoration is acceptable. It is even possible that some
make-good was done in the factory before sale.
£4000–£6000

MINTON c.1845
Height 10½ins: 26.8cm No mark.
A fine vase after a Sèvres original, well painted with exotic birds and with blue, pink and gilt handles and borders. The type is known as Sneyd, number 301, from the design record books and was on view at the 1849 Birmingham Exhibition.
Pair £2000–£3000

MINTON 1862
Height 4¾ins: 12cm Painted name and impressed date code.
An unusual pair of vases in pale and dark green and with white lily of the valley flowers.
£350–£500

MINTON 1862
Height 16ins: 40.6cm Printed ermine mark.
A pair of well painted vases in bright enamels, the *bleu-céleste*
ground with fine tooled gilding. The pair were shown at the 1862
London Exhibition and bear the puce ermine mark used only on
such pieces.
£2500–£3000

MINTON1867

Height 11½ins: 29cm Impressed name and PODR.
An unusual vase with matt and burnished acid-etched gilt borders and ovals against a mirror-black ground. The Acid Gold Process rights were bought by Minton in 1863. The quality is high but black is a very difficult colour to sell. In blue £250–£300.
£180–£250

MINTON 1870

Height 10½ins: 26.6cm Impressed name with date code.
A pair of moon flasks with brightly painted flowers against a turquoise ground. Although decorative, the market is unkeen on moon flasks, particularly when resting on stubby feet, as here. The quality is breathtakingly high and they deserve to be more highly priced.
£1500–£2000

MINTON 1871
Height 20ins: 50.8cm. Impressed name and date code.
A pair of vases with brightly enamelled birds reserved on a too-dark blue ground. The birds in their naturalistic landscape look as if they had been copied straight from a book rather than having been adapted to fit the format.
£3000–£5000

MINTON 1871;
Height 14½ins: 37cm Impressed name and date code.
An important clock garniture in pâte-sur-pâte by Louis Marc Emmanuel Solon. Solon came to England from Sèvres in 1870, having worked there for twelve years. He had this garniture ready for the London International Exhibition in 1871. An engraved illustration appeared in the *Art Journal Catalogue*. It was an extremely expensive set to produce: modelling £20, moulds £5 and Solon's work £40, about £8000 in today's terms.
£15000–£20000

Probably MINTON 1871
Height 10ins: 25.4cm Impressed name and blurred date code.
A Chinese moon flask form which was very popular in the 1870s and 1880s. Compare the shape with the less elegant vases on page 262. Here the naturalistic fish have been painted against the inevitable turquoise ground. This form has been seen with the small loop handles broken off, the stubs ground down and patches restored.
£400–£600

MINTON 1873
8¼ins: 20.8cm Impressed marks and date code.
A pair of vases based on the Chinese *cong* form and probably to a design of Dr Christopher Dresser. The cloisonné-style decoration is in coloured enamels and the ground colour is the ever-present turquoise.
£600–£900

MINTONS, possibly 1875
Height 7⅞ins: 17.1cm Printed name and retailer's mark, blurred date code.
This garniture is a brilliant display of Minton's ability to cope with the most difficult of ceramic designs. The thinly potted vases have a rose-pompadour ground well painted with putti and gilt-edged panels. The top half is fine gilt trelliswork which would have resulted in considerable kiln losses, leaving few perfect examples for the decoration stage. It has to be said, however, that the overall appearance is none too comfortable. Nevertheless, they would, because of their delicacy and subject matter, sell extremely well. £2500–£3500

MINTONS c.1880
Height 6½ins: 16.5cm Printed impressed names.
These vases are an object lesson in how a design can fail. The shape is squat, the silvered and gilt flowers are thin and badly placed. The bronzed bands and handles are taken from Chinese *famille-rose*, *famille-verte* and Canton vases of the period which are now firmly disliked. They also lack their covers. It is strange that a factory such as Minton could consider making vases such as these when they were capable of such superb examples as those on pp264.
£250–£300

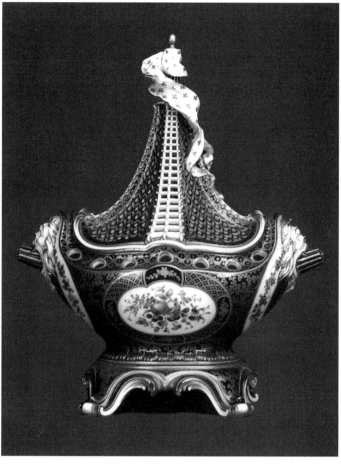

MINTONS 1887
Height 15½ins: 39.5cm Printed gilt crowned globe and impressed date code
A superb coloured pâte-sur-pâte vase by L.M. Solon, signed, with an elaborate design of putti being weighed. The borders in green, yellow, brown and gilding. The technique of pâte-sur-pâte was extremely slow and fraught with dangers of failure and was expensive at the time. This vase is particularly successful and the subject matter easier to take than many of Solon's designs.
Pair £5000–£7000

MINTON 1878
Height 18ins: 46cm Impressed and printed marks including date code and retailer's mark of John Mortlock & Co, London 1879.
A bone china 'Vaisseau à Mât' or 'Pot Pourri en Navire' as the Sèvres archives record it. Modelled in two parts and based (loosely) on a ship's mast and rigging it is painted on one side with a rustic village scene after David Teniers the Younger and on the other with flowers. Both in the 18th century when the originals were created and when the 19th century copies were made, the figure subject would have been the 'front', the flowers the 'back'. Taste has changed and a private owner might well reverse the sides.
£6000–£8000

MINTONS c.1890
Height 6ins: 15cm No mark.
A small moon flask with a pâte-sur-pâte panel by T. Mellor, signed and inscribed 'after A. Boullemier'. The body is in sage and pink with blue ribbons, the white figures against midnight-blue. Thomas Mellor was one of Solon's pupils and his identifiable work uncommon, additionally it is rare to have the name of the artist who drew the design recorded. Mellor was not, however, another Solon, the left hand putto is particularly weak.
Pair £800–£1200

MINTONS 1894

Height 8¾ins: 22.2cm Impressed name and date code.

A rare L.M. Solon vase with a white figure in pâte-sur-pâte against the 'artificial ruby' ground which changes colour according to the light in which it is viewed. Bichromate of potash and alumina and green or blue produce pink under artificial light or deep carmine at night. £1800–£2500

MINTONS 1902

Height 9 ins: 23cm Printed crowned globe, impressed date code.

A pâte-sur-pâte vase by Alboin Birks and with his monogram. Birks' skill in foliage was marginally better than Solon's but his figures were somewhat tubby. £1200–£1800

MOORE 1873

Height 8ins: 20.3cm Impressed PODR.

Despite the mixture of Rococo putti with Japanese-style bird painting, this fan vase would sell readily. £300–£400

MOORE 1875
Height 6¾ins: 17.2cm Impressed name.
This vase – *'pot pourri a vaisseau'* – as it appears in the Sèvres records, was a popular target for the Victorian porcelain manufacturers and appears also by Minton, see page 266 and Royal Worcester. This Moore example is a miniature and lacks the top of the mast.
£300–£500

MOORE c. 1895
Height 4ins: 10.2cm Impressed name.
A pair of vases in the form of epiphyllum cacti, a favourite form, not only of Moore's but also of other factories in the last quarter of the 19th century. The flowers are pale yellow and the bases gilt. They can be found in other sizes, 6ins: £400–£600; 8ins: £600–£800.
£200–£300

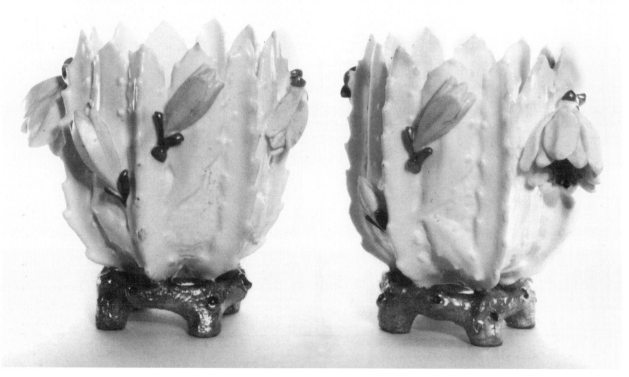

ROCKINGHAM 1826-1842
Height 5¾ins: 14.5cm Printed griffin in puce.
A well painted vase with typical early 19th century flowers including the popular ranunculus and passion flower reserved in a gilt-edged panel on a green ground. Numerous English factories made similar vases, not all of which are identifiable. Similar Staffordshire vases have been noted with added Rockingham marks.
£400–£600

ROCKINGHAM 1830-1842
Height 10¾ins: 27.2cm. Printed griffin in puce.
A curious vase with an assemblage of contemporary influences including the crane handles which are taken from Canton vases. It could have been a disaster but works well.
£700–£900

SPODE First quarter of the 19th century
Height 4½ins: 11.5cm Painted name.
A typical Japan pattern of the period loosely based on Imari with the usual flowers and fenced garden. Brightly coloured, good quality spill vases have risen rapidly in price.
£600–£900

SPODE c.1820-1830
Height 10¼ins: 26cm Painted name.
A fine and rare pair of vases in neo-Classical style, well painted with named scenes of mythological subjects. The handles are gilt and the whole of good quality. Figure subjects are much rarer than flower painting at this date. The shape is identified in the Spode pattern book as no.35 'New Shape French Jar' and came in nine sizes.
£3000–£4000

SPODE 1965
Height 13½ins: 34.2cm Gilt printed marks including name.
A limited edition vase of reasonable quality with a wealth of detail about Sir Winston Churchill's life and honours and issued in the year of his death. Like most limited editions it has collapsed from £100-£150 in 1975 to its present £150–£250.

SWANSEA 1819
Height 4½ins: 11.5cm Painted name.
A rare pair of documentary spill vases entertainingly painted with antelope in oriental style. They are signed MM for Mary Moggridge and dated 1819. They were sold at Sotheby's in 1973 to Sir Leslie Joseph for £520. When his collection was sold in 1992 they fetched over £8000.

WEDGWOOD 1920s
Height 7¼ins: 18.5cm Printed vase and name.
A pair of vases with plum and gilt dragons against a pale runny blue ground. The thin background makes the dragons better delineated than is usual, hence a higher price. Pairs are much less common than singles but, in contradiction to normal practice, little more expensive than two singles. £500–£600

WEDGWOOD 1920s
*Height 9½ins: 24.2cm Printed vase
and name, pattern no. Z4968.*
This print of *Butterfly women* is not
common and when seen is rarely
well coloured or registered. Here
the dress is blurred and the whole
over-dark. A good clear design
would make £2000–£2500.

WEDGWOOD 1920s
Height 16½ins: 41.9cm Printed vase and name, pattern no. Z4968.
An exceptionally large Fairyland vase with a brightly coloured
pattern *Imps on a Bridge and Tree House*. The shape is rare.
£3000–£4000.

WEDGWOOD c.1930
Height 11ins: 28cm Printed vase and name.
This pair of trumpet vases has coloured butterflies against a
mottled blue ground. As with dragon lustre, not expensive
compared to Fairyland. Given the same size, any other form of
vase with a similar design would fetch the same, £400–£600
pair.

WORCESTER, FLIGHT, BARR AND BARR c.1813-1815
Height 12ins: 30.5cm Printed name.
A fine ice pail vase with a deep blue ground and gilt scrolls and handles. One side is painted with flowers, the other with shells, almost certainly by Thomas Baxter. Shells are now the most popular of subjects and the more naturalistic the painting, the more they fetch.
£6000–£8000

WORCESTER, FLIGHT, BARR AND BARR c.1813-1820
Height 6½ins: 16.5cm Printed name.
A blue ground urn with a panel of Faith, pair to Hope. Scenes of a religious nature are not good sellers, worse than almost any other subject. Those of female saints, such as this, are best, male saints middling, crucifixions and entombments worst. This form can be found on a high pedestal. Same form with landscapes £3000–£4000, shells £6000–£8000. This one £2000–£3000.

WORCESTER, FLIGHT, BARR AND BARR c.1815
Height 8½ins: 21.5cm Painted name.
A vase and cover with gilt snake handles and a deep blue ground. The panel is painted by 'Dr.' George Davis with an exotic bird in a landscape. In the early 19th century, Davis painted many vases in the style of the 1770s, often on a blue scale ground. His birds are more akin to James Giles' work than that of the Worcester factory but can be identified by the over-filling of the space available. The flame knop is characteristic of the period and used by no other factory.
£1500–£2000

WORCESTER, FLIGHT, BARR AND BARR c.1820
Height 7ins: 17.8cm Printed name.
A superb urn with a deep blue ground painted with fine quality flowers. Although only 7ins high it gives the impression, particularly in the photograph, of being much larger.
£1000–£1500

WORCESTER, KERR AND BINNS 1858
Height 8¾ins: 21.3cm Printed shield and date.
A high quality pair of vases painted in grey with titled portraits of classical authors, the rest with tooled gilding. Kerr and Binns period Worcester is still underpriced, possibly due to the small quantities available. The subjects here are a little doleful, attractive girls would raise the price by half as much again.
£600–£800

WORCESTER, KERR AND BINNS c. 1860
Height approx. 4ins: 10cm Printed shield.
A pair of spill vases with classical heads in grey, the ground deep blue with gilt wreaths.
£500–£600

ROYAL WORCESTER
1862
Height 7ins: 17.8cm Printed crowned circle and date code.
A pair of vases and covers painted in white enamel by Thomas Bott with Grecian heads against a turquoise ground. Bott's work is invariably of a high standard and here the shapes with their gilt Bacchic handles work well with the decoration.
£1000–£1500

275

ROYAL WORCESTER 1863
Height 6ins: 15cm Printed crowned circle, date code.
A rare Parian flower holder with unusual pink, purple, brown and green coloration picked out in gilding. A good quality piece which would appeal more to the decorator than the Worcester collector. The form derives from the Greek rhyton drinking cup, but here probably owes more to the early 19th century glass and ormolu flower vases.
Pair £300–£400

ROYAL WORCESTER 1866
Height 12ins: 30.5cm Printed name.
A fine vase with a deep blue ground enamelled in white by Thomas Bott with putti in 'Limoges' style. He exhibited from 1851 (on glass) to 1870 when he died, leaving a son, Thomas John, who worked at Worcester in the same style from 1873 to 1885/6. The enthusiasm for earlier works of art, which began in earnest in the middle of the 19th century, led to a Middle Ages/Renaissance revival covering all the applied arts. The source of Bott's work was the mid-16th century Limoges enamelled copper in Mannerist style. In the 19th century they were amongst the most expensive works of art.
£1200–£1800

ROYAL WORCESTER 1867 and c.1870

Height 6¾ins: 17.2cm Impressed and printed crowned circle, one with date code.

A comparison showing the same form treated in different ways. The example on the left has painted coloured flowers, gilt borders, turquoise medallions and white beads, £250–£300; the other has pale apricot ground and gilt borders, £180–£250. The left-hand example is also more sharply moulded. Our 20th century eyes might find vases held by chopped-off chicken legs difficult to stomach, but in the last century there were no such qualms and the less edible bits of animals were made into jewellery (fox and rabbit feet); inkwells (goat and horse hooves) and hat ornaments (dead birds).

ROYAL WORCESTER 1872

Height 8¼ins:21cm Printed crowned circle mark and dated 1872.

A good pair of Japanese-taste vases after James Hadley with portraits tinted against a bronzed ground by James Callowhill, the handles and feet also bronzed and gilt. These and similar pieces were exhibited at the London International Exhibition of 1871-72 and were illustrated in the *Art Journal*. The standard of production is very high and it is surprising that Japanese style wares have still not received the recognition they deserve. £1200–£1800

ROYAL WORCESTER last quarter of the 19th century
Height 9ins: 22.8cm Printed crowned circle, PODR.
An elephant vase after a model by James Hadley. The animal has a brown howdah with brightly enamelled details picked out in gilding. A popular, uncommon and amusing beast which can be found in a variety of colour schemes: white £300–£500; white and celadon £500–£800; peach/yellow and gilt £600–£800. This example £800–£1200.

ROYAL WORCESTER c.1875
Height 10ins: 25.4cm Impressed crowned circle, PODR.
A rarer model than the elephant and again by James Hadley, as usual bearing his moulded signature. The camel is sage green and with gilt details. Coloured example £500–£600.
£400–£600

278

ROYAL WORCESTER 1876

Height 3¼ins: 8.5cm Printed crowned circle and date code.
A most entertaining little vase, probably inspired by a Japanese
bronze original. The reptile is bronzed and gilt against the lemon-
yellow ground. Uncommon and still underpriced.
£80–£120

ROYAL WORCESTER 1879

Height 7⅞ins: 20cm Printed crowned circle, date code.
An amusing spill vase with the owl in two tones of gold and well
executed. Owls are always popular. The use of bamboo was nothing
new, Wedgwood had used it in the 18th century and the Chinese
in the 17th.
£150–£200

ROYAL WORCESTER 1879

*Height 11½ins: 29.3cm Printed crowned circle, date code and retailer's
mark 'Tiffany and Co. New York'.*
A well-produced moon flask with matt coloured and gilt flowers,
the moulded handle and base with silver (actually platinum) and
gilding. Sadly, the floral decoration is stiff and ill-placed. The
addition of Tiffany's mark helps the price by about 20%.
£350–£500

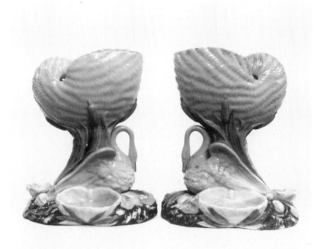

ROYAL WORCESTER 1880
Height 3⅛ins: 8cm Printed crowned circle, date code.
A multiple vase after an oriental original with a crudely-coloured spray of prunus attached to interlocking sections of bamboo. An amusing idea poorly executed.
£150–£200

ROYAL WORCESTER 1880
Height 8ins: 20.3cm Impressed crowned circle mark, date code.
A pair of shell vases palely-tinted in pink and green and reminiscent of Belleek. An uncommon form.
£400–£600

ROYAL WORCESTER 1880
Height 11ins: 28 cm Printed crowned circle, PODR date code.
The prunus blossom background on this pair of vases is transfer-printed in grey and over painted with brightly-enamelled and gilt butterflies and plants. The result is attractive and unusual, but outside the field of most Worcester collectors and therefore underpriced.
£400–£600

ROYAL WORCESTER 1880

Height 15½ins: 39.5cm Printed crowned circle and date code.
A large and rare pair of Japanese taste vases modelled by James Hadley whose moulded signature appears on one. The figures are in relief and coloured, apparently carved from a section of bamboo and almost certainly copied from contemporary Chinese bamboo carvings.
£1800–£2000

ROYAL WORCESTER 1881

Height 11ins: 27.9cm Impressed and printed crowned circle, date code.
A shell wall pocket with gilt coral branch suspension. A difficult object to display in a cabinet and, as most collectors are not prepared to fix them to a wall as intended, they are relatively inexpensive.
Pair £250–£350

ROYAL WORCESTER 1882

Height 8ins: 20.3cm Printed crowned circle, date code.
An attractive moon flask with a bright yellow body and well coloured with mauve clematis and printed gilding. Compare this with the moon flask (page 279).
Pair £600–£800

ROYAL WORCESTER 1884
Height 14½ins: 37cm Printed and impressed crowned circle, date code.
A pair of vases and covers in Eastern taste, the flowers in tones of gilding on a matt ivory ground, the covers pierced. These vases are often found without covers. This is not always obvious from the examination of the mouth, which is gilt as if no cover was called for. The only reliable way is to check the shape number on the base with the list of shapes in Sandon (see Bibliography), to see if they were made with them. Some vases still appear in proportion without the covers (which in this case are too large anyway) and are readily saleable. Lacking covers this pair £600–£900.
£800–£1200

ROYAL WORCESTER 1888
Height 23½ins: 59.7cm Printed and impressed crowned circle, date code.
A large, brilliant and rare example of the best that the Victorian factories could produce. The original of this vase was modelled by James Hadley and it bears his moulded signature. The decoration is finely gilt on an ivory-coloured ground and with brightly-enamelled peacocks. The vase was made for R.W. Binns, the firm's art director and his monogram appears on the base. Vases of this quality appear infrequently on the market and are always ready sellers.
£3000–£5000

ROYAL WORCESTER 1896
Height 19ins: 48cm Printed crowned circle, date code.
A large and decorative vase of good quality, painted with shaggy-looking flowers against the usual peach/yellow ground. The scrolling on the shoulders in relief on sage-green.
Pair £1500–£2000

ROYAL WORCESTER 1890
Height 7ins: 17.8cm Printed crowned circle, code for 1890.
A vase and cover pierced by George Owen, lacking his signature, but unmistakable. A pencil note on the base records that there are 2,034 perforations, all of which were cut, according to contemporary accounts, without guide lines. While Owen's work apparently falls into the same category as Chinese concentric ivory balls, the Lord's Prayer on a grain of rice and chain link carved from a single piece of wood – craftsmanship as opposed to art – his work does seem to fall on the right side of the divide. This success lies in the simplicity of the piercing and limited colour or gilding. Where this has been abandoned and the piercing is accompanied by flower or landscape painting, the result is a disaster.
£3000–£5000

**ROYAL WORCESTER
c.1897**
*19¼ins: 49cm Printed shape no.
2419 and registered no. 369944
and crowned circle mark.*
A fine pair of vases painted
and signed by (William A.)
Hawkins, who was also known
for portraits and figure subjects.
He was foreman of painters at
the factory for many years. The
still lifes are reserved on a
green ground and with, as
usual, superb gilding. Minor
restoration to wings on the
handle would not dent the
price a great deal.
£4000–£6000

ROYAL WORCESTER 1897
Height 10ins: 25.5cm Printed crowned circle and date code.
This peach, yellow and gilt swan has a vase between the wings. A
decorative and usable object which comes as a variation with a
putto holding a rein on the tail.
£600–£800

HADLEY, WORCESTER 1897-1900
Height 9¾ins: 24.7cm Printed mark.
Typical of Hadley's Worcester with the use of coloured clay slips
which look remarkably like polychrome bubble-gum or putty. His
wares were generally of good quality and are best when they depend
purely on their form and colour, as here. However, the contrast
between the white and the dark colours is not in favour. Had it
been painted with flowers, £400–£600.
£250–£350

ROYAL WORCESTER 1899
Height 8ins: 20.3cm Printed crowned circle, PODR and date code.
A well-painted pair of vases by C(harles). Baldwyn, signed, with a greenfinch and a chaffinch on gorse and apple blossom and with gilt details. A change from this artist's usual swans and showing the skill of which he was capable.
£1800–£2500

ROYAL WORCESTER 1900 and 1907
Height 16½ins: 42cm Printed crowned circle.
A comparison between two vases of the same form, treated in different ways. The left is painted with chrysanthemums, the moulding of pale tone and with gilding, £300–£400; pair £800–£1200. The other has Highland cattle painted by John Stinton, signed, the rest of the body a gold-speckled, greenish bronze, £800–£1200; pair of second £2000–£3000.

ROYAL WORCESTER 1900
Height 8ins: 20.3cm Printed crowned circle.
This vase and the next are as close as English porcelain ever got to the Art Nouveau Movement, although it flowered profusely in pottery. In neither case would it be recognised by the Continental purist. This is actually quite a successful vase but it would not sit happily with the peachy/yellowy vases of most collectors.
£180–£250

ROYAL WORCESTER 1901
Height 12ins: 30.5cm Printed crowned circle, date code.
A slightly nearer attempt at Art Nouveau than the last with aquilegia/colombine in enamels and gilding and with gilt tendril handles. Pair £400–£600

ROYAL WORCESTER 1902
Height 5ins: 13cm Printed crowned circle, date code.
A very simple, but typical 'Japanese' design first produced in 1874 and still being produced nearly thirty years later.
Pair £100–£200

ROYAL WORCESTER 1903
Height 3½ins: 9cm Printed crowned circle, date code.
A small bulb pot with the lily leaf feet coloured in greenish-reddish gold 'Shot Enamels'.
£100–£150

ROYAL WORCESTER 1907
Height 8ins: 20.3cm Crowned circle, date code and Sabrina Ware.
Sabrina Ware was Royal Worcester's attempt at 'art' pottery. It was made from 1897 to 1930 in the Parian body with simple decoration (here stencilled), its effect depending on the purposely uncontrolled glaze and colour effects. It has to be said that, compared to the likes of Pilkington's Royal Lancastrian or Bernard Moore, it was hardly successful. It is rare, however, and it has its devotees. Better examples can make £300–£400.

ROYAL WORCESTER 1907
Height 9½ins: 24.5cm Impressed and printed crowned circle, date code.
A pair of vases of Persian-influenced form with pierced wing handles and painted by C(harles).H(enry). C(lifford). Baldwyn, signed, with swans against a soft blue sky. Baldwyn's swans are perennial favourites. £2500–£4000

ROYAL WORCESTER 1907
Height 21ins: 53cm Printed crowned circle, PODR, date code.
A superb pair of vases with apple-green bodies and white relief scroll-work. The scenes were painted by W(illiam). A. Hawkins, signed, after Boucher. They are titled on the base 'Summer' and 'Autumn'. Vases of this quality now very rarely appear on the market and fetch high prices when they do.
£4000–£6000

ROYAL WORCESTER 1908
Height 11¼ins: 28.5cm Printed crowned circle with date code.
Signed pairs of vases by the Stintons are now very expensive. These do not have the very best colouring and gilding the factory was capable of. Unlike the previous vases, these would look incomplete without their covers.
£1800–£2500

GRAINGER, LEE & Co., WORCESTER c.1825-1830

8¼ins: 20.8cm Painted mark and titles.

A rare pair of vases painted with what at the time would have been the wonders of the age: Brighton Pavilion and the New London Bridge. The rest of the body is smothered with *schneeballen*, the tiny mayflowers copied from Meissen. The base is painted to imitate marble. They have suffered some damage but were sold at auction in 1986 for a remarkably low £400.
£600–£900

ROYAL WORCESTER 1909
Height 5⅛ins: 13cm Printed crowned circle, date code.
A small vase painted by E(rnest). Barker, signed, with a coal tit.
Small vases with bird painting are always popular.
£250–£300

ROYAL WORCESTER 1910
Height 10¾ins: 24.5cm Printed circle and date code.
A goblet vase painted by H(arry). Martin, signed. Painting of this
kind was a standard product and despite (or perhaps their
familiarity makes them a 'safe' buy) the numbers available they are
ready sellers.
£300–£500

ROYAL WORCESTER 1912
Height 7½ins: 19cm Printed crowned circle mark and date code.
An uncommon style of decoration of a type made from the turn of
the century until the 1930s. The factory was trying new lines, most
of which were commercial failures and were not produced in bulk.
An interesting and unusual collection could be made of these
rarities. In this example the transfer-printed outlines of the
chinoiserie scenes are brightly enamelled within panels on a grey
simulated-granite ground.
£500–£700

ROYAL WORCESTER 1913
Height 8⅝ins: 22cm Printed crowned circle, date code.
A rare pierced vase and cover, originally a Grainger shape of about
thirty years earlier, with angel heads and scrolls supported on an
osprey and coloured peach/yellow.
£400–£600

ROYAL WORCESTER 1917
Height 5ins: 12.6cm Printed crowned circle, date code.
A quite well pierced vase in Grainger style, painted by James
Stinton, signed, with a pheasant. The Royal Worcester factory
continued Grainger shapes after they bought it out in 1889.
£250–£400

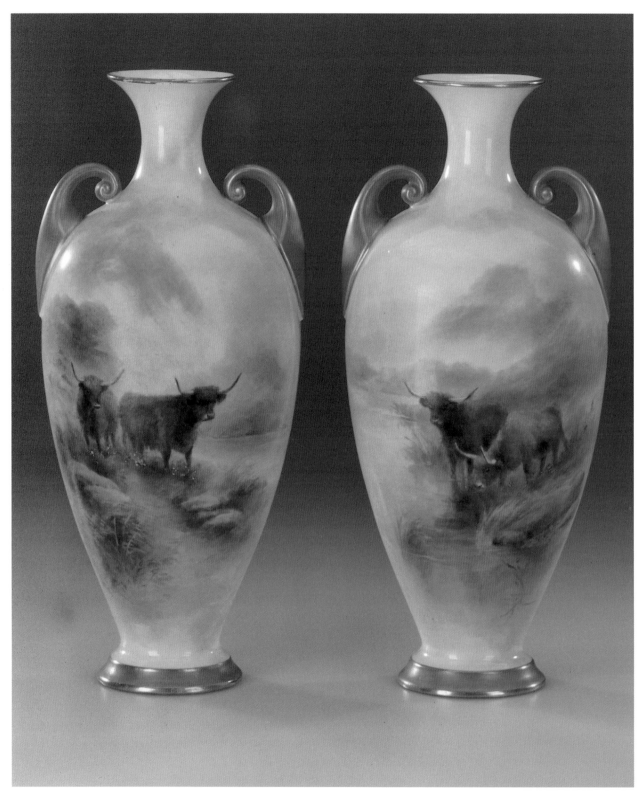

ROYAL WORCESTER 1909
Height 7¾ins: 19.75cm Printed marks, date code and shape no. 287A/H.
A pair of vases with the perennially favourite Highland cattle by Stinton, signed. They rose to fame in the mid-1970s and have remained popular ever since. Interestingly, if one looks back to the Sotheby's Belgravia catalogues of the period, the prices are, in real terms, unchanged and, in actual terms, the same as ten years ago. £1000–£1500

UNATTRIBUTED c.1835

8ins: 20.2cm Unmarked.

A pair of spill vases of ice-cream cone form attractively painted with flowers on a bright blue printed, berried sprig ground. The shape is a bit dull and a flared mouth would have made them a great deal more appealing, nevertheless they are very interior-decoratory and saleable. £450–£650

ROYAL WORCESTER 1921
*Height 8¾ins: 22cm Printed crowned circle,
date code.*
Although uncommon, these vases painted
by Ernest Barker, signed, would not be
strong sellers for several reasons: the scenes
are too small, the pastel tones of the gilt
border are too weak and the gilding rubbed.
Barker's sheep are quite as good as Harry
Davis', but generally less expensive.
£600–£800

ROYAL WORCESTER 1923
*Height 8¼ins: 21cm Printed crowned circle,
date code.*
A pair of vases painted by Harry Davis,
signed, with his usual sheep in a landscape.
Although sheep were his stock-in-trade,
each painting was newly conceived and his
works are extremely popular.
£1500–£2000

ROYAL WORCESTER 1926
Height 8ins: 20.2 cm Printed crowned circle, date code.
Despite the scarcity of Royal Worcester wares influenced by
Wedgwood's Fairyland lustre, they are not expensive. The colours
here are green and the brilliant flame-orange known as 'tango',
which immediately slots any piece bearing it into the 1920s or
1930s, and gilding. The process is a mixture of hand painting and
transfer-printed outlines with a printed gilt key block.
£300–£500

UNATTRIBUTED first quarter of the 19th century
Height 3½ins: 9cm No mark.
One of a pair of spill vases of middling quality. The ruined abbeys
are typical of the period when 'gothick' was all the rage. However,
the painting is a mite amateur and the gilding uninspired. The
beading at the foot is here part of the mould, unlike the hand-rolled
beads used by contemporary Worcester (see page 273).
£350–£500

MINTONS 1874
Height 12½ins: 31.8cm. Impressed 1348, potting codes and date code.
One of a pair of Mintons bone china, 'cloisonné' designs after Dr Christopher Dresser of the 1870s; these are, in fact, based on Chinese patterns. The Japanese cloisonné industry was in its infancy and was, at the time, only copying Chinese examples. The design shows Dresser's grasp of the Japanese idiom; it is not a straight copy of an actual example but overlays various elements of the oriental design vocabulary. £1200–£1500

MINTONS 1873
Height 8½ins: 21.5cm Printed crown and globe mark, impressed MINTONS, potting numbers and date code.
Another Dresser design, this time combining a classical ewer form with 'cloisonné' decoration. As almost always, the turquoise blue is strongly in evidence. It is prone to crazing and flaking away from the body and all these cloisonné design pieces should be protected from a wide range of sudden temperature changes. £500–£700

UNATTRIBUTED early 19th century
Height 4ins: 10cm No mark.
A spill vase of better quality than that on page 295 in both painting and gilding. These small vases cry out for there to be a pair, which is worth four times a single.
£200–£300

UNATTRIBUTED 1830-1840
Height 4ins: 10 cm No mark.
A spill vase with an amusing scene of a sultan and courtesan. The previous vase is continuing the 18th century style of landscape painting, whereas this is rooted in the 19th century genre style. There was a short-lived enthusiasm for Moorish designs in the 1840s and this vase probably dates from then, although the form is early 19th century.
£250–£400

FAKES AND FORGERIES

The terms 'fake' and 'forgery' tend to be used indiscriminately as if they are synonymous, whereas it would be better to follow the earlier, distinct meanings. A Fake is a genuine object that has been altered in some way, such as adding decoration or a mark. A Forgery is a fresh, deliberate attempt to deceive.

The collector of 19th century British porcelain has an easy time of it as far as any form of deception is concerned. The original quality is generally so high and the body and decoration so distinctive, that there is almost no chance of a forgery being attempted. Not only are the skills no longer available, but even if they were, the cost in time and effort would outweigh the return. In the second half of the century, several Continental manufacturers made wares which were 'in the style of' Worcester, if not out and out copies. They were usually not marked, but New York and Rudolstadt used a mark very similar to Worcester's (a crown over RW in a lozenge). None of the pieces comes close to any of the English factories and very little experience is needed to dismiss them.

The greatest problem (and even here it is minimal) is with added marks. A Carltonware lustre vase has had its mark erased, probably with hydrofluoric acid, and a Wedgwood mark substituted (see below). It is a reasonably well executed fake but, being on earthenware, not porcelain, would be unlikely to fool any collector. A bird group with a fake Dorothy Doughty mark was noted in the first edition of this book. Considering the crash in the market for Doughty birds, this deception now

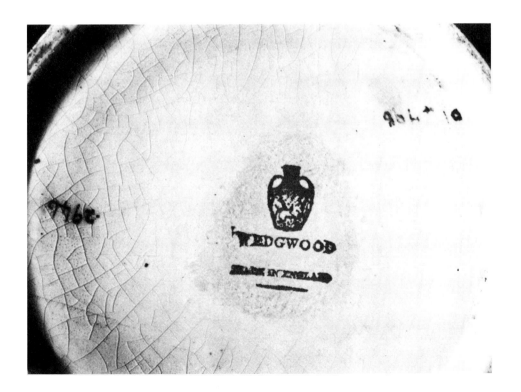

Factory A teapot

Red Spode mark added
to the Factory A teapot

A COFFEE CUP, c.1840-1845, probably Coalport
This cup, with its highly translucent clean white body is enamelled with 'dry blue' flowers. The entwined twig handle and gilt dentil have been taken from Sèvres, as has the painting which is found on Vincennes porcelain of c.1750-55. The base has the Sèvres factory mark of interlaced Ls, but the calligraphic nature of their painting is characteristic of 19th century copies. Coalport received a ticking-off from Joseph Marryat in *A History of Pottery and Porcelain*: 'We regret to have observed upon some recent specimenns of (Coalport) manufacture, marks of double L and anchor', in imitation of Sèvres and Chelsea.
£10–£15; with saucer and unworn £30–£60

DEPARTMENT OF WISHFUL THINKING.
6¾ins: 17.1cm
This figure was bought at a car boot sale. It is modern, probably German, and in hard paste porcelain. The mark has been painted on in ink and the base given a thick layer of lacquer. No such figure or mark exists and such a deception would seem unlikely to fool anyone. As with restoration, resorting to a pin or a tooth tap will immediately disclose the soft layer of paint or lacquer.

looks decidedly unwise. The pair of Paris hard paste porcelain vases (page 303) shows a degree of combined invention and stupidity which one can only admire. One vase has had a crudely transferred crowned circle mark added and the other has a genuine mark cut from a damaged piece and stuck on to the base.

The Grainger's Worcester ewer (page 305) is an oddity. The original mark has been ground away. This has left shallow depressions, visible in the photograph as light streaks from the bottom left corner up to the pattern number. The faker, for some bizarre reason, probably lack of research, has created a mark that does not exist – it should read 'Royal Worcester England' (page 306). This fake dates back twenty years when Grainger's Worcester and the main factory were widely apart in value. Now that Grainger's has risen to approach Royal Worcester, such an exercise would not be worth while. In most cases, when a mark has been removed or when another has been substituted, the glaze is recreated by clear nail varnish or a similar colourless lacquer. The smell of pear drops can linger for months and the nose is a sense which the porcelain collector should cultivate. (See also Damage, page 309.)

Bill Coles has kindly brought to my attention the Factory A teapot (page 300) which has had a red Spode mark added in paint under a clear lacquer.

The bases of a Spode cup decorated on the inside with gilt leaves on a deep blue band, circa 1820-25, and a replacement Copeland's saucer bearing a date code for 1903 (page 307) show that services were in use for getting on for a century. The making of tea plates, when they came into fashion in the 1880s, to match an earlier tea service, is not uncommon and the practice of putting on the original pattern number can be confusing.

Emile Samson of Paris, well-known reproducer (not forger!) of much English and other 18th century porcelain, made very little in the way of copies of 19th century porcelain. However, he or someone else made reproductions in hard paste of Swansea and Nantgarw. So, also, did Coalport, who were probably responsible for the plate illustrated on page 308. The mark is typical of most forgeries – it is far too deeply impressed and legible. Most Nantgarw marks are barely visible. Other forgeries have the additional letters C.W. (China Works), but these marks are in too large a typeface. The plate is also too heavily potted and the quality of the painting leaves much to be desired. The forger invariably leaves, unintentionally, some small clue to his deception and each object is best approached with the words: 'You are a forgery, prove to me you are right.'

Finally, it must be said that many of the major English factories were, in the 19th century, not above making copies of 18th century English and Continental porcelain. Coalport, Copeland, Brown-Westhead, Moore, Bevington, and Minton all produced pieces that could have been mistaken for products of the 18th century Continental factories, usually Sèvres. This was almost always done for the best possible reasons – flattery is the greatest form of compliment. Other pieces were made as replacements to Sèvres services or were copies made to special order. Nevertheless, there is still a slight suspicion that some pieces were made with a deliberate attempt to deceive.

A pair of Paris hard paste vases with false marks

a

b

c

Not strictly a forgery, but the kind of problem which might cause a double-take for the inexperienced. It was common practice for porcelain factories to make copies or replacements for services, not only English but also Oriental and Continental (see page 302). These, as with the Swansea example, might be half a century later. The practice continued through the 19th century. The most commonly encountered example is the making of tea plates post-1870 to match teasets, still in use, which lacked them. This splendid dessert plate (a), dating from the 1830s, has had a companion (b) made c.1880. The match is superficially good, but the crazing seen on the earlier, softer bone china is absent on the later piece (c). The replacement maker did not have moulds that matched the indented rim of the original. Additionally, the flower painting had deteriorated by the last quarter of the 19th century, becoming thinner and flatter. This also applies to the gilding, which lacks the richness of its progenitor.

Original £200-£300, later £100-£150

Grainger's
Worcester ewer

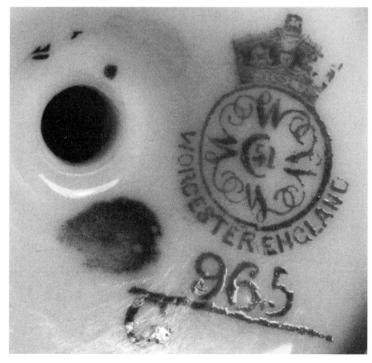

Fake mark on ewer

Genuine Royal Worcester marks

Spode cup c.1820-25 and replacement Copeland's saucer, 1903

Coalport plate with forged Nantgarw mark

Forged Nantgarw mark

DAMAGE

The question of damage raises a number of problems and personal preferences. Some collectors, if they cannot find a perfect example, would rather have a damaged piece looking as near to its original condition as possible. To achieve this, the modern restorer has developed an extraordinarily high standard of workmanship. Epoxy resin adhesives, kiln-hardened enamels and skilled painters can produce nearly undiscoverable repairs that do not yellow with age and are hard to the touch. They do, at the moment, show under ultra-violet light and feel dead when touched on the teeth – no doubt even this will change. When buying from a shop, it is vital to ask whether the piece is in any way restored and to insist on a receipt that states its date, factory and condition. A reliable shop will be only too happy to do this. Hesitation or refusal should put you on your guard.

The Worcester figure of a water carrier illustrates a method of cleaning up a cracked or chipped base with a technique more commonly associated with glass. The base has been ground smooth on a carborundum wheel until it appears perfect when viewed standing, although a little flat, but it exhibits a curious change of plane at one point on the underside, arrowed in the photograph below.

TECHNIQUES
BODIES

HARD PASTE

The clay mixture used to produce a porcelain object is known as the 'paste' or 'body'. The Chinese developed what is now called 'true' or 'hard paste' porcelain in about the 7th century A.D. It was formed of a mixture of petunse, a ground feldspathic rock, and kaolin, a refractory white clay. During firing at about 1350°C, the rock melts to a glasslike substance which is held in shape by the clay. The glaze is fired at the same time and becomes one and the same with the body. The result is a material that is translucent, tough, resists chipping and cracking and gives a musical note when struck. The exact mixture varied through time and other ingredients were often added. It was the same mixture of kaolin and china-stone (nothing to do with Stone China) that Böttger discovered at Meissen in 1709 and was used later at most other Continental factories.

SOFT PASTE

Beginning with the short-lived Medici factory in Florence in the third quarter of the 16th century, many European factories attempted to make porcelain without knowing the secret ingredients – the arcanum, as it was called. The obvious route, which most of the seekers took, was to include ground glass with the clay. This could produce a breathtakingly beautiful body – as it did at Sèvres and Swansea – but it was very unstable in the firing. Or, to be strictly accurate, firings. A first firing was at about 1100°C to 1200°C and a second at around 900°C for the glaze. The wastage at the first stage was great, with many pieces ending up as a molten blob on the bottom of the kiln. For this reason, the factories expended an enormous amount of effort to try and find a translucent body which fired over a wide temperature. These differing mixtures are lumped together under the term 'soft' or 'artificial' paste.

ENGLISH HARD PASTE

The 18th century English factories such as Chelsea (which included glass in the mix), Bow and Lowestoft (which included bone ash) and Worcester (which included soaprock) are typical of the attempts to stabilise the paste. Each had advantages and disadvantages. There was also the partly successful, although financially disastrous, attempt at hard paste by William Cookworthy at Plymouth in about 1768, which transferred to Bristol in 1770. In 1774 Richard Champion took control.

Champion's patent was sold to a group of Staffordshire potters in 1781, the fledgling New Hall company. Their hard paste body was fired first at a high temperature and then a second time at a lower temperature for the glaze, thereby combining elements of both hard and soft paste techniques.

The hybrid hard paste bodies were used at several factories around the end of the 18th century and the beginning of the 19th, some of which are still unidentified.

The English hard paste body is a rather dirty grey colour and includes a mass of minute air bubbles. No doubt it was this and the increasingly popular earthenwares that brought about another change of paste. This was a harking back to the Bow/Lowestoft magic ingredient – bone ash – but now combined with clay and china-rock.

BONE CHINA

This modified hard paste was bone china, still the quintessential English body. It rapidly overhauled all other English formulae and the majority of objects in this book were made in it. Nevertheless, each factory had its own mix and this altered over time. The variations are a help and a hindrance. On the one hand, a factory might have made ten slightly different bodies, all of which look a little different and on the other, the variations are specific to that factory, allowing attributions to be made. Some were less successful than others. The Derby paste around 1820-30 has an ill-fitting glaze which crazes and discolours. Several factories around 1870 used a mixture which renders plates made in it to crack concentrically, often as a result of thermal shock – see below.

PARIAN

The realisation by Sèvres that their figures came out of the kiln at the biscuit stage looking like marble led them to develop a range of models sculpted specially to take advantage of this discovery. While Sèvres was greatly influential on many of the 18th century English factories, biscuit figures did not take hold in the way they did in France. One reason was the small scale of the figures of which the English factories were capable, the other was the rough and absorbent nature of their biscuit. It very rapidly became dirty and stained, and cleaning was extremely difficult, if not impossible. Nevertheless, some factories did attempt it successfully, Derby, Rockingham and Minton being the most obvious examples. It was Minton which inherited the biscuit mantle, producing nearly two hundred different models from the 1820s. In the early 1840s they, and Copeland and Garrett, introduced a new body, both claiming that they were first. Copeland named theirs Statuary Porcelain and Minton called theirs Parian after the marble from Paros. Wedgwood called theirs Carrara.

The new body was a modified hard paste. It included a third to two thirds of feldspar. This had the effect of reducing the firing temperature from about 1350°C for ordinary hard paste to about 1100-1200°C, thereby saving greatly on firing costs. By the middle of the century huge numbers of figures were being produced, many being reductions from full size marbles. The Art Unions, lotteries which gave works of art as prizes, bought large numbers for their subscribers. To a limited extent Parian (it was Minton's name which stuck) was used for the making of useful objects, jugs being the most common. It was vases and plaques in the Parian body which Solon used for pâte-sur-pâte and which proved so much more satisfactory than the hard paste that he had used while at Sèvres.

Models were slip-cast and therefore display in their interiors a smoother reflection of the outside detail. Many carry titles, the sculptor's name, dates and manufacturer's name, and often a date code as well.

WARES

The earliest method of producing a pottery vase or jug was to build up the form using thin 'sausages' of clay and winding them round and round a base. Almost all primitive societies have used this method, and some still use it today. The invention of the wheel led to more sophisticated forms and thinner walls. In the 18th century, wares such as plates and cups were formed in a mould on a wheel. In the former, the lump of clay is placed on the mould which forms the inside of the plate. A profile of the finished shape is pressed into the revolving lump of clay, thereby producing the bottom of the plate. The technique is known as jiggering and is still in use. Cups are produced in a similar fashion, but here the profile forms the interior of the cup. The machine is known as a jolly.

Wares can also be cast. Plaster of Paris moulds in two or more parts are taken from the original, fitted together and filled with liquid clay, known as slip. The plaster absorbs water leaving a film of clay nearest to the mould. Surplus slip is poured off and the film allowed to dry until it can be freed from the mould. At this 'leather' or 'green' stage it dries further until ready for the kiln.

FIGURES

The earliest prehistoric figures were modelled individually by hand, but this was a laborious and inefficient technique. Moulds taken from an original will enable a number of copies to be made without loss of definition. The earliest method was to produce a two part mould and hand press a sheet of clay into each half, cutting off the surplus at the edges. Removed from the mould, the two halves of the figure were luted together with slip and, at least in the better examples, the mould line smoothed away. The piece was then fired. This method of producing figures was used at Meissen (which is why their figures seem heavy) and in Staffordshire for many pottery figures. Slip casting (see above) was introduced for figures in the 18th century and continues as the most frequently used technique.

Most figures will need several moulds – the most complex twenty or thirty. Each limb, head, dog, musical instrument or whatever has to be assembled by the 'repairer' after removal from the mould, using slip as the adhesive. Mould lines will be smoothed away on the better examples. In many cases the work of the repairer is not then finished, as extended arms and so on need support in the kiln if they are not to sag. Pillars of the same clay support the limb, shrinking at the same rate as the figure. Shrinkage can be up to a third of the original height.

UNDERGLAZE BLUE

In the first half of the 14th century, the Chinese discovered that cobalt under the glaze produced a blue colour. Along with the less reliable copper red, it was the only colour that would withstand the firing temperature. It was used on soft paste at the Medici factory in the 16th century and reappeared in the late 17th century at Rouen and St Cloud. Meissen employed it to a limited extent, as did Chelsea. It featured at most of the 18th century English factories, often transfer-printed under the glaze (see below) and has continued as one of the cheapest and most popular decorative styles.

ENAMEL COLOURS

The Chinese developed overglaze enamel colours in the 15th century. Enamels are effectively ground glass with a flux which melts at a lower temperature than the glaze. The different colours have different melting points and a polychrome painted object may have to be fired several times, reducing the temperature at each firing. As the enamels and the glaze of soft paste mature at very similar temperatures, the colouring appears to sink into the glaze, giving a soft, sensitive appearance. On hard paste, such as Meissen, the enamels do not blend with the glaze and stand proud of it, often enough to feel. The effect is hard and brilliant.

Enamels were almost invariably hand-painted until the 20th century when chromolithographic transfers took over. With very few exceptions, enamel colours are permanent and cannot fade, the main exception being a turquoise blue, which can oxidise and turn brown. If the firing has not achieved a sufficient temperature, the enamels may not have bonded to the body sufficiently and may flake off. The same problem may be encountered if the coefficients of expansion are not properly matched. The problem was at its most acute in the 1860-80 period. The collector looks at the obvious place for restoration – the rim – and may overlook flaked enamels on the body of the piece which can be matched by a skilled restorer.

GILDING

The gold used to decorate ceramics is always 22 carat. The proud boast on some cheap and nasty 20th century Continental crockery that it is 'Guaranteed Genuine 22 carat Gold' is wasted – it couldn't be anything else.

The gold can be applied in two forms. The earliest was to grind gold and honey together, paint this on and fire at a low temperature. The result was a thick, rich gold which could then be tooled, as was common at Sèvres. In the 1770s mercury gilding largely superseded honey gilding. An amalgam of gold and mercury could be painted on and fired. The heat drove off the mercury (causing the rapid demise of kiln-workers, as it was very poisonous), leaving a thin, brassy body.

Minton developed acid gilding in 1863, see page 161. The mass-produced 'Collectors' plates advertised in the Sunday colour supplements frequently boast that the design is 'lined in gold by hand'. It would be, since this is still cheaper and quicker than applying it mechanically. However, complex designs were occasionally transfer printed, as were the outlines of Fairyland lustre.

PRINTING UNDERGLAZE

Cobalt blue could be hand-painted under the glaze but a speedier process was developed in England in the mid-18th century. A copper plate was engraved with the required design as if for an ordinary print on paper, but deepening the cut. A pull was taken on tissue paper using a hot cobalt-containing ink, which would mature in the firing to blue. The tissue was then rubbed down on to the biscuit-fired piece. The tissue could be washed off once the ink had dried or it could be fired on, burning away in the kiln and leaving the design behind. The piece was then glazed and fired again, producing an underglaze blue transfer print.

Underglaze printing can be distinguished from hand painting by close examination, preferably with a lens, of the blue tones. With painting, an area of tone will be achieved by graduating the blue by means of more or less colour on the brush. In a print the tone is achieved by engraving lines, close together or cross-hatched. The denser the engraving, the darker the blue will be.

PRINTING OVERGLAZE

Transfer printing was also done over the glaze using the same technique. The result was much sharper, as the design was not blurred by the depth of glaze but was less permanent, as it was prone to scratching and wear from cutlery or washing. Often the overglaze pattern was used as a key for hand painting. Overglaze engravings appear mostly composed of fine lines.

This method of obtaining an overglaze print on to porcelain had two variations:

(1) Bat-printing. The copper plate, which had the illustration formed of thousands of tiny dots tapped into it with very light hammer blows, was charged with linseed oil. The 'bat', which was a thin sheet of flexible jelly-like glue cut to the size of the required print (usually about 2 x 3ins or less), was applied to the copper plates and withdrawn, taking with it the design in barely visible oil. This was then pressed on to the ware. The sticky oil, now on the object, was dusted with colour, usually black, and then fired. The result was an extremely finely detailed print. The drawback was that the pattern was even more subject to wear than was the overglaze transfer engraving and perfect examples are now uncommon. Occasionally the bat-print served as the underlying detail for hand-colouring. Bat-printed designs appear made up from minute dots of colour.

(2) Pluck and dust. This technique combines elements of transfer printing and bat printing. A tissue pull is taken from the deeply-engraved copper plate, not in ink but in oil. This is applied over the glaze to the object and dusted with colour. It produces a thicker image, but is also subject to wear. The appearance is of coarse dots and lines.

A technique which took its inspiration from book illustration was block printing. Here, a wood-cut or wood engraving was inked in whatever colour was needed, printed on to transfer paper and applied to the required surface, more usually earthenware rather than porcelain.

In the chromolithographic process, the required image is drawn in a greasy crayon on to a finely-grained, flat stone. The stone is wetted and the required colour, also oily in nature, is applied with a roller. The colour sticks to the drawing on the stone but is repelled by the wetted areas. A tissue paper pull can then be taken in a press. A different stone will be needed for each colour. The technique is still in use today but with metal replacing the stone and the image being produced on it photographically.

CLEANING

The majority of 19th century porcelain was made to be used. Little damage can be caused to it by washing in detergent and hot water. This is best done in a plastic bowl away from the sink to avoid hitting the sink or the taps. Dry with a tea towel. Heavily flower-encrusted pieces should be doused in detergent and sprayed with a shower spray until clean, tickling with a small house-painting brush to dislodge dirt from crevices if necessary. They should be allowed to drip-dry or be dried with a hair dryer. Vases with an iron joining rod should be separated first. Iron will rust and may split the piece.

Some bone china, particularly from the first half of the century, may be crazed and discoloured. In some cases this discoloration can be reduced or removed by immersing the piece in hot water containing a lot of biological washing powder and some water-softening powder in a plastic bowl. If the bowl can be kept warm for several hours, or overnight, so much the better. In the vast majority of cases, the piece will be transformed after a final wash. Be warned, however, that on rare occasions the problem may be made worse. There will be no problem on hard pastes or Parian, nor on bone china from the last quarter of the 19th century onwards. The matt, pale turquoise from the third quarter of the 19th century which discolours brown may prove fugitive.

USAGE

As stated above, most ceramics were made for use and, if used intelligently, can continue to be used. However, there are some problems. Bone china may be crazed and each crack is a pathway for liquids and dirt to penetrate. Vases which are crazed should not be used for flowers unless another container for the water is inserted. Plates can be used for their original purpose but should be washed immediately to prevent gravy or fruit acid getting into the body. Gilding and, to a lesser extent, enamels, will suffer from the scratching of cutlery. Tea and coffee services can also be used but cracked and crazed examples should not. Making tea or coffee in the original pots is just a little too risky, as they may crack. On no account should fruit, cheese or butter be left in containers overnight – oils, once in, cannot be got out.

Dishwashers are banned, as they remove gilding and the high temperatures at which they work can cause thermal shock.

Some bone china (mostly plates) of the second half of the 19th century had a built-in time bomb. Stresses inherent in the manufacture can cause spontaneous cracking, often concentrically around the foot rim. Rapid changes in temperature can exacerbate the risk. Dangerous positions are on a windowsill where a winter's chill and central heating can alter the temperature quickly. Using excessively hot water when washing-up, or putting a plate of cheese in the refrigerator are also risky. While these problems are rare, they are worth consideration.

19TH CENTURY BRITISH & IRISH
PORCELAIN FACTORIES

1. **S. Alcock & Co.**, Cobridge, c. 1828-53, Hill Pottery, Burslem, 1830-59.
2. **Belleek Pottery**, County Fermanagh, Ireland, 1863 to present day.
3. **John Bevington**, Kensington Works, Hanley, 1872-92.
4. **E.J.D. Bodley**, Hill Pottery, Burslem, 1875-92.
5. **W. Brownfield & Son**, Cobridge, 1850-91.
6. **Brown-Westhead, Moore & Co.**, Cauldon Place, Hanley, 1862-1904, later **Cauldon**.
7. **Cauldon**, Shelton, Hanley, 1905-20.
8. **E. & C. Challinor**, Fenton, 1862-91.
9. **R. Chamberlain**, Worcester, 1783-1840, later **Chamberlain & Co.**
10. **Chamberlain & Co.**, Worcester, 1840-52.
11. **Coalport (Caughley)**, Coalport, Shropshire, 1795 to present day.
12. **W. T. Copeland & Sons**, Spode Works, Stoke, 1847 to present day.
13. **Copeland & Garrett**, Spode Works, Stoke, 1833-47, later **W. T. Copeland**.
14. **Davenport**, Longport, 1793-1887.
15. **Derby**, 1750-1848, 1878 to present day. **Bloor Derby** 1830-40, **Derby Crown Porcelain Co. Ltd.** 1876-90, **Royal Crown Derby Porcelain Co. Ltd.** 1890 to present day.
16. **Doulton & Co.**, Burslem, 1882 to present day. **Royal Doulton** from 1901.
17. **W. H. Goss; Goss and Peake**, Falcon Pottery, Stoke, 1858-1944.
18. **G. Grainger & Co.**, Worcester, 1839-1902.
19. **Grainger, Lee & Co.**, Worcester, 1812-39, later **G. Grainger & Co.**
20. **J. Green**, retailer, London 1834-74.
21. **J. Hadley & Sons**, High Street, Worcester, 1896-1905.
22. **Hill Pottery**, see **S. Alcock**.
23. **G. Jones**, various addresses in Stoke, 1864-1957.
24. **Kerr & Binns**, see **Worcester**.
25. **C. Meigh**, Old Hall Pottery, Hanley, 1835-61.
26. **Minton**, Stoke, 1793 to present day.
27. **Moore Brothers**, St. Mary's Works, Longton, 1872-1905.
28. **Nantgarw**, Glamorgan, Wales, c.1813-14 and 1817-22.
29. **New Hall Porcelain Works**, Shelton, Hanley, 1781-1835.
30. **Paragon**, Longton, 1920 to present day.
31. **Robinson and Leadbeater**, Stoke, 1864-1924.
32. **Rockingham Works**, Nr. Swinton, porcelain manufacture 1826-42.
33. **J. Spode**, Stoke, c. 1784-1833, later **Copeland & Garrett**.
34. **Swansea**, 1814-22.
35. **J. Wedgwood**, various addresses, 1759 to present day.
36. **Worcester, Dr. Wall**, c. 1751-83; **Flight**, 1783-92; **Barr** and **Flight & Barr**, 1792-1807; **Barr, Flight & Barr**, 1807-13; **Flight, Barr & Barr**, 1813-40; **Kerr & Binns**, 1852-62; **Royal Worcester Porcelain Co. Ltd.**, 1862 to present day.

BIBLIOGRAPHY

Aslin, E., *The Aesthetic Movement*, London, 1969

Atterbury, P. and Batkin, M., *The Dictionary of Minton*, Antique Collectors' Club, 1990

Barnard, J., *Victorian Ceramic Tiles*, London, 1972

Batkin, M., *Wedgwood Ceramics 1846-1959*, London, 1982

Battie, D. (ed.), *Sotheby's Concise Encyclopedia of Porcelain*, London, 1990

Berthoud, M., *A Compendium of British Cups*, Bridgnorth, 1990

Blacker, J. F., *19th Century English Ceramic Art*, London, no date

Brayshaw Gillespy, F. and Budd, D. M., *Royal Crown Derby China*, London, 1964

Cushion, J. and M., *A Collector's History of British Porcelain*, Antique Collectors' Club, 1992

Drakard, D. and Holdway, P., *Spode Printed Ware*, London, 1983

Emmerson, R., *British Teapots and Tea Drinking*, HMSO, 1992

Eyles, D., *Royal Doulton 1815-1965*, London, 1965

Eyles, D. and Dennis, R., *Royal Doulton Figures*, Stoke-on-Trent, 1978

Des Fontaines, Una, *Wedgwood Fairyland Lustre*, London & New York, 1975

Godden, G. A. *Encyclopedia of British Pottery and Porcelain Marks*, London, 1964; *An Illustrated Encyclopedia of British Pottery and Porcelain*, London, 1966; *Coalport and Coalbrookdale Porcelains*, London, 1970; *Victorian Porcelain*, London, 1970; *Mason's China and the Ironstone Wares*, Antique Collectors' Club, 1980; *Staffordshire Porcelain*, London, 1983; *Ridgway Porcelains*, Antique Collectors' Club, 1985; *Chamberlain-Worcester Porcelain*, Wigston, 1992

Haggar, R. and Adams, E., *Mason Porcelain and Ironstone*, London, 1977

Henrywood, R. K., *Relief-Moulded Jugs 1820-1900*, Antique Collectors' Club, 1984

Holgate, *New Hall and its Imitators*, London, 1971

Jewitt, L., *Ceramic Art of Great Britain*, London, 1972

Jones, A. E. and Joseph, Sir L., *Swansea*, Cowbridge, 1988

Jones, J., *Minton*, Shrewsbury, 1993

Lockett, T. A. and Godden, G. A., *Davenport*, London, 1989

Miller, P. and Berthoud, M., *An Anthology of British Teapots*, Broseley, 1985

Pugh, P. D. Gordon, *Staffordshire Portrait Figures of the Victorian Era*, Antique Collectors' Club, 1988

Reilly, R. and Savage, G., *The Dictionary of Wedgwood*, Antique Collectors' Club, 1980

Reilly, R., *Wedgwood, The New Illustrated Dictionary*, Antique Collectors' Club, 1995

Rice, D. G., *Rockingham Pottery and Porcelain*, London, 1971; *English Porcelain Animals of the 19th Century*, Antique Collectors' Club, 1989

Sandon, H., *Royal Worcester Porcelain*, London, 1973; *Flight and Barr Worcester Porcelain 1783-1840*, Antique Collectors' Club, 1978

Sandon, H. and J., *Grainger's Worcester Porcelain*, London, 1989

Shinn, C. and D., *Victorian Parian China*, London, 1971

Whiter, L., *Spode*, London, 1970

FACTORY INDEX